FOUL DEEDS AND SUSPICIOUS DEATHS AROUND WIGAN

TRUE CRIME FROM WHARNCLIFFE

Foul Deeds and Suspicious Deaths Series

Staffordshire and The Potteries
Colchester
Manchester
Guildford
Derby
Northampton
Pontefract and Castleford
Tees
Bedford
Bristol
Carlisle
Newcastle
Southend-on-Sea
Barnsley
Birmingham
Blackburn and Hyndburn
Chesterfield
Coventry
Ealing
Guernsey
Huddersfield
Leeds
Liverpool
Newport
Nottingham
Rotherham
London's East End
Wigan

More Foul Deeds Wakefield
Mansfield
Leicester
Stratford and South Warwickshire
Brighton
Folkestone and Dover
Oxfordshire
Black Country
Durham
Bradford
Cambridge
Halifax
Scunthorpe
Barking, Dagenham & Chadwell Heath
Bath
More Foul Deeds Birmingham
Bolton
More Foul Deeds Chesterfield
Croydon
Grimsby
Hampstead, Holborn and St Pancras
Hull
Lewisham and Deptford
London's West End
Norfolk
Portsmouth
Warwickshire
York

OTHER TRUE CRIME BOOKS FROM WHARNCLIFFE

Norfolk Mayhem and Murder
The A-Z of London Murders
Unsolved Murders in Victorian and
    Edwardian London
Unsolved Yorkshire Murders
A-Z Yorkshire Murder
Brighton Crime and Vice 1800-2000
Essex Murders

Executions & Hangings in Newcastle
    and Morpeth
Norwich Murders
Unsolved Norfolk Murders
Yorkshire's Murderous Women
Black Barnsley
Durham Executions
Strangeways Hanged

Please contact us via any of the methods below for more information
or a catalogue.

WHARNCLIFFE BOOKS
47 Church Street – Barnsley – South Yorkshire – S70 2AS
Tel: 01226 734555 – 734222 Fax: 01226 – 734438
E-mail: enquiries@pen-and-sword.co.uk
Website: www.wharncliffebooks.co.uk

Foul Deeds & Suspicious Deaths Around

WIGAN

Mike Fletcher

Wharncliffe Books

This book is dedicated to my mum,
Lilian Margaret Fletcher
1931-2006

First published in Great Britain in 2007 by
Wharncliffe Books
an imprint of
Pen & Sword Books Ltd
47 Church Street
Barnsley
South Yorkshire
S70 2AS

Reprinted in 2009

ISBN 978 1 84563 040 9

A CIP catalogue record for this book is available from the
British Library

Typeset in Plantin and Benguiat by
Phoenix Typesetting, Auldgirth, Dumfriesshire

Printed and bound in England by
CPI UK

Pen & Sword Books Ltd incorporates the imprints of Pen &
Sword Aviation, Pen & Sword Maritime,
Pen & Sword Military, Wharncliffe Local History, Pen and
Sword Select, Pen and Sword Military Classics and Leo
Cooper.

For a complete list of Pen & Sword titles please contact
PEN & SWORD BOOKS LIMITED
47 Church Street
Barnsley
South Yorkshire
S70 2AS, England
E-mail: enquiries@pen-and-sword.co.uk
Website: www.pen-and-sword.co.uk

Contents

Acknowledgements

I must offer my sincere gratitude and appreciation to the hardworking staff of the Wigan History Shop, as it is with their tireless efforts and goodwill that this book has been written. Much of the research was based on the reports which have appeared in Wigan's newspapers through the years; anyone seeking to learn more about Wigan's murders and crimes would be advised to spend time studying the back copies of the *Wigan Observer* and *Wigan Examiner* on microfilm at the Wigan History Shop.

I would also like to thank the staff of Wharncliffe Books for their assistance in this project. Particular credit should go to series editor, Brian Elliott, as without his support and encouragement this book would never have been written.

Introduction

This is my second book on Wigan. Whereas *The Making of Wigan* concentrated on the town's evolution, *Foul Deeds & Suspicious Deaths Around Wigan* takes a look at the darker side of Wigan's past, concerning some of the most notorious murders that have occurred throughout the town's long and varied history. Taken together, at first glance it might appear as though Wigan was a town filled with murderers, but that would be an extorted view.

Wigan gained much more status and evolved into a recognised town during the late medieval era. For instance, in 1246, a charter from the king made Wigan a royal borough and the town had the right to hold a weekly market. From 1258 the market was held twice a week and the town gained an annual three-day fair. By 1297, Wigan began to return MPs to Parliament.

Wigan was regarded as a respectable town, and yet it was a dangerous place, too. In 1315 it was attacked by rebels led by Sir Adam Banastre and Sir William de Bradshaigh, lord of Haigh. This tale of rebellion and deceit also includes Wigan's earliest murder and is recounted in Chapter 1: *Mayhem & Murder*.

Wigan continued to develop into the reign of the Tudor and Stuart monarchs. Although the seventeenth century saw the genesis of the town's textile trade, it also witnessed death and destruction within the spectre of civil conflict. Wigan played a pivotal role within the region throughout the three campaigns of the English Civil War, resulting in an endless series of skirmishes between Parliamentarian and Royalist forces as they indulged in a violent game of tug of war over the town's control.

The eighteenth century was a time of massive change and had a great deal in store for Wigan, especially with the expansion of its early mining activities – and the creation of the first cotton mills. Transport also played a significant role in the modernisation of the town, initially with the introduction of turnpikes, though more significantly with the navigation of the River Douglas and the cutting of both the Lancaster Canal and the Leeds & Liverpool Canal. Wigan underwent significant rebuilding and modernisation during the Hanoverian period,

This page and opposite:
The Industrial Revolution brought great changes to Wigan, with the rapid expansion of mining, the establishment of its cotton mills, and the creation of its transport network.

and yet, despite such improvements, the eighteenth and early nineteenth century was also a time of violence, with Wigan suffering at the hands of the Jacobites in 1745, for example. This was also a time of robbery, with highwaymen, like Up Holland's George Lyon, preying on the unsuspecting traveller – a story told in Chapter 17, *The Highwayman's Haunt*.

By the nineteenth century the Industrial Revolution was in full flow, with Wigan at the heart of the new technology, emerging as one of Lancashire's most important industrialised towns. During this period it was home to countless cotton mills and, literally surrounded by collieries, took on the image of a dirty, smoky and heavily polluted town. The arrival of the railways saw Wigan become a major transport hub for the region and, as people flooded into the town in search of work, its population boomed, resulting in massive overcrowding and squalor amongst its poorest residents.

Because so many of the murders in this book are concentrated in the second half of the nineteenth century, Victorian Wigan appears to be a very violent place in which to live, but this has to be taken in context. It's true to say that Victorian Wigan was a hard, working-class town, but it was also plagued with the same problems that many other similar-sized towns faced. Poverty was rife almost throughout the borough, and matters were exacerbated by the Cotton Famine of 1861–5, when mill workers were laid off in their thousands, forcing the poorest families to go without food. Employment was high but wages were low, and workers were forced to endure intolerable working conditions. The worst slums were concentrated in the centre of town, particularly in areas such as Scholes. Diseases such as cholera, smallpox and typhus reached almost epidemic proportions. Wigan's Dispensary was opened in 1798 but health care was practically non-existent. Wigan Infirmary opened many years later, in 1873. All of these factors influenced the manner and attitude of the population and, in extreme cases, created 'ideal' conditions for murder.

Mindless feuds between rival families are common even today, though they rarely result in murder – though that was the outcome of one such feud told in Chapter 3, *Feuding Families*. However, it was a disagreement within the family that led to someone's death in Chapter 14, *Incest & Murder*.

Although there was full employment, poverty was widespread and, for many families, the final resort was the workhouse. Wigan's Union workhouse on Frog Lane was home to around 1,000 inmates at any one time, many of them children who had often been born within the workhouse and had known no other life. Chapter 4, *A Scalded Child* tells the tale of the short life of one workhouse child.

Wigan was one of the largest mining towns on the South Lancashire Coalfield and the town's many collieries employed the vast majority of the adult male population; as well as many boys. Many of the murderers featured in these cases are colliers. They are, by the very nature of their employment, a hardy breed — men plunged deep into the bowels of the earth in search of 'black gold' were often heavy drinkers and prone to violence – and Wigan's colliers were noted as being amongst the hardest on the South Lancashire Coalfield. Wigan's collieries attained national significance in 1863 with *The Wigan Murder* (Chapter 2).

Domestic violence, mostly husbands beating their wives, often went too far and resulted in murder. Circumstances like these feature in cases like *Without Provocation* (Chapter 10), *Possessed by the Demon Drink* (Chapter 8), *The Case of the Hindley Collier* (Chapter 18) and *Kicked to Death* (Chapter 5). Mostly, such cases involved a husband attacking his wife, though the notable exception is in the case of *The Odd Confession* (Chapter 9) when it was the common-law wife who murdered her husband. Although in the case of *The Wasteful Wife* (Chapter 15), the murdering husband was as sober as a judge, excessive drinking was a common factor in almost all of these domestic violence cases. The low price of alcohol led to drinking to excess and became the preferred 'escape' of the working classes. In towns like Wigan there was, quite literally, a pub on every corner! Apart from domestic violence, fighting or 'purring' in the street was a common occurrence and could have fatal consequences. A notable scuffle which got out of hand is recalled in *Street Fighting* (Chapter 12).

The Wigan Constabulary, formed in January 1836, had John Whittle as its head constable and, with just five constables under his command, struggled to cope with the town's rising crime rate. Significant improvements were made following the appointment of William Simm in 1852 as Wigan's first chief constable, the number of constables dramatically increased and better working practices were introduced. And yet, even towards the end of the nineteenth century, Wigan's Victorian police force often found itself overstretched and struggled to cope with the amount of criminal activity occurring in the town.

It was common practice to call upon the support and expertise of neighbouring forces in times of crisis, and it was under these circumstances that an officer from the Salford force lost his life in Wigan, recounted in *The Murder of a Detective* (Chapter 13).

Murder is often a crime with the most powerful of motives, though equally it can be a mindless and totally unnecessary act of violence, having no motive at all. Two of the cases in this book recall seemingly motiveless murders, and surprisingly, in both cases the crime takes place in a remote, rural setting. In *The Moss Brook Farm Incident* (Chapter 7) a man is beaten to death with a poker, while in *The Ackhurst Hall Murder* (Chapter 6) a mysterious stranger bludgeons a young girl to death. Murder is hard to justify regardless of the circumstances, but the murder of a child is indefensible. Two of the most disturbing cases recorded here involve the murder of young children: in the case of *The Rape and Murder of a Child* (Chapter 11), the disappearance of a young girl results in the discovery of her body at the bottom of a disused mine shaft, and the arrest of her stepfather; and in the case of A *Child Murderer* (Chapter 20) the residents of 1950s' Wigan live in fear as their town is stalked by a mysterious serial killer who preys on young boys.

They say that the course of true love never runs smooth, but then again they also say that vengeance is a dish best served cold! Lovers often quarrel and many love affairs end in tears, but few lovers bear a grudge for months, secretly waiting for the right moment to pay their ex-lover back for jilting them, but that is exactly what occurred in *A Jilted Lover* (Chapter 19). And similarly, in *The Body in the Canal* (Chapter 16) it's the ex-husband who murders his ex-wife.

These stories provide us with a fascinating insight into the lives of Wiganers through the ages, as each case involves the experiences of seemingly ordinary people, who, through changing circumstances, commit murder.

CHAPTER 1

Mayhem & Murder

1315–23

Two knights fought, Sir William was the victor, while Sir Osmund lay dead.

I t's perhaps easy to think that the medieval period was a time of great lawlessness, where the nobles and gentry held both power and rights over the common man and were therefore able to get away with committing crimes – even murder. Although England was at times a turbulent place in which to live, with crime, poverty and starvation the ever-present backdrop, and wars and rebellions often on the horizon, there were laws; and if these were broken, punishment would be handed out, irrespective of the status of the perpetrator.

During the medieval period Wigan was a small, though prominent town. The charter of 1246 had made the town one of only four royal boroughs within Lancashire, and had aided its economy by establishing a weekly market. Law and order was controlled by the Court Leet, and the town was patrolled between the hours of dawn and dusk by specially appointed watchmen. By the reign of Edward I Wigan had increased its national status by returning two representatives to Parliament. However, despite the benefits which representation undoubtedly brought to the town, this privilege soon proved too expensive to continue and was terminated within a few years. Wigan was then controlled by a small number of highly influential people, including Sir William Bradshaigh, who had acquired the Haigh estate in 1285 through his marriage to Mabel Norris.

Although Wigan was a well administrated town, the same level of good governance could not be said for the county as a whole. Lancashire was controlled by Thomas, Earl of Lancaster, a feeble character who, following King Edward's defeat at Bannockburn in 1314, had acquired power and influence well beyond his status. The role of keeping his barons under

Haigh Hall, 2005. The original Haigh estate had been created by the Norris family though passed to Sir William Bradshaigh in 1285 through his marriage to Mabel Norris.

control fell to the Earl's right-hand man, Robert de Holland, who misused this power and behaved as a tyrant to barons and tenants alike. The mistreatment of the barons had only one result . . . rebellion.

The catalyst for this regional insurgency was his handling of Sir Adam Banastre, the manorial lord of Shevington. There had been feuding between the two families for many years and this just proved to be the last straw. Sir Adam, supported by Sir Henry Lea of Park Hall and Sir William Bradshaigh of Haigh, led his followers on a merry rampage throughout the county during October and November 1315. Their wanton spree began with the murder of Sir Henry de Bury, a close friend of de Holland, and resulted in attacks upon Clitheroe Castle, Knowsley Hall, Liverpool Castle, Warrington, Halton Castle near Runcorn, and Manchester, before returning to Wigan on 2 November.

Once they were fully rearmed, the rebels turned their attention to Preston, and it was here, in a valley at Deepdale on 4 November, that they were finally defeated by a combined force led by the Deputy Sheriff of Lancashire, Sir Edmund de Neville and Sir Robert de Holland. Although both Banastre and Lea escaped the battlefield they were later captured and executed for their crimes at Leyland on 11 November. Sir William Bradshaigh on the other hand avoided capture and was never found.

Meanwhile, back at Haigh, Mabel had assumed her husband had been killed and carried on her life without him. In the years that followed, a Welsh knight, Sir Osmund Neville, befriended Mabel and asked for her hand in marriage. She refused. With this rejection, Sir Osmund informed her that Earl Thomas had granted him the right of the Haigh estate, and should she not consent to marriage, she would be evicted from her own estate. Mabel had little option and reluctantly agreed to marry Sir Osmund. However, in spite of Osmond's threats and seemingly unlimited power, it would later transpire that this odious knight had in fact lied: the Earl had never promised him possession of the Haigh estate, and was never likely to.

Meanwhile, the king decided to pardon Sir William Bradshaigh in his absence, on 21 May 1318. Nevertheless, despite this declaration being circulated far and wide, there was no response from Sir William. As the months and years went by, Mabel concluded that her husband must surely be dead.

Matters between Earl Thomas and the king continued to deteriorate. The final straw was Earl Thomas's defeat at the hands of the Scots at the decisive Battle of Borrobrigg in the spring of 1322, where the Earl was captured, tried for treason and later executed at Pontefract Castle in Yorkshire. The victorious Scots overran the English, penetrating as far south as Preston.

Sometime afterwards, while Mabel was offering food to the poor gathered outside the gates of Haigh estate, she saw a man amongst the crowd, dressed in the attire of a knight, a hood covering his face. As she offered him bread, he drew back the hood, and there before her was her missing husband, Sir William. Mabel was shocked and upset at his sudden appearance, thinking for years that he had died on the battlefield. At this point, Sir Osmund appeared, and seeing his wife taking an interest in this stranger, mercilessly attacked her, beating her severely. Sir William threatened to kill Sir Osmund for attacking his wife, deceiving her and as a direct result stealing his estate.

When Mabel was offering food to the poor gathered outside the gates of Haigh estate, she saw a man amongst the crowd, dressed in the attire of a knight, with a hood covering his face . . . who turned out to be her missing husband.

This old picture postcard of Standishgate shows Mab's Cross in its original position – a location it retained until 1921, when it was moved to its present position, across to the opposite side of Standishgate in the grounds of Mab's Cross Primary School.

Sir Osmund, fearful of Sir William's reputation and what he would now do to him, immediately fled for his life. Sir William wanted revenge and pursued him some distance before finally catching up with him near Newton. It was here that the two knights fought. Sir William was the victor. Sir Osmund lay dead. The site where this confrontation and subsequent murder took place is located not far from the gates of Newton Park at modern-day Newton-le-Willows, and is marked by a large red boulder, known locally as the 'Blood Stone'.

Sir William Bradshaigh was convicted of the murder of Sir Osmund Neville, and banished for a period of 'a year and a day'. Mabel was also punished for her bigamous marriage to Sir Osmund. Her penance was severe: henceforth she would have to walk barefoot, from her home at Haigh to the wayside cross on Standishgate, once a week, for the remainder of her life. This was indeed harsh punishment, as in those times the roads, particularly those between Haigh and Wigan, were little more than dirt tracks, hard and dusty during the dry summer months, and wet and muddy throughout the winter. Indeed, to reach Wigan she would have to cross the River Douglas, and the only means was by the old ford, a daunting task at the best of times. When Sir William finally returned from his term of exile in 1323, he had vengeance on his mind and a score to settle with the de Hollands. By now Sir Robert had been imprisoned, and Sir Richard de Holland was the head of the family, and both he and Sir William, who had joined forces with Thomas Banastre, clashed on several occasions. With matters looking as though it might result in yet another rebellion, the king visited Wigan in October 1323. He had both de Holland and Bradshaigh arrested. Feeling that Bradshaigh was the guiltier culprit, he sequestered the manor of Blackrod from him and refused to return it until Sir William agreed to end this mindless feuding. Reluctantly, Sir William agreed to end this campaign of violence against the de Holland family, and the king, true to his word, returned to him the manor of Blackrod without further penalty.

Back at Haigh Hall, Sir William and Mabel lived a happy life together. Sir William died in 1333, and Mabel five years later. The couple were buried side-by-side in the family chapel at the parish church. The story of Mabel's agonising weekly journey to the wayside cross became the stuff of legend, and the cross itself acquired the name Mab's Cross. It remained at

Two images of Wigan Parish Church, taken at the beginning of the twentieth and twenty-first centuries. Following the deaths of Sir William and Mabel Bradshaigh the couple were buried side-by-side in the family chapel at the parish church.

its original position on Standishgate until 1921 when it was moved across to the opposite side of the road to stand in the yard of the Wigan Girls' High School. Mab's Cross survives to the present day – though only its worn base remains – within the school yard of the aptly named Mab's Cross Primary School.

CHAPTER 2

The Wigan Murder

1863

. . . as one of the officers inspected one of the mine's furnaces he made a grim discovery . . .

igan, particularly during the Victorian era, was a major coal mining centre. Collieries, both large and small encircled the town, and their mountain-like spoil heaps formed an almost natural skyline. Coal mining was the single largest employer, and as a result of the 1842 Mines & Collieries Act, forbidding women from working underground, coal mining was a male dominated occupation. Despite being a tightly knit community, disagreements between fellow miners were inevitable, and fights not unusual, though murder amongst miners was something else altogether.

The Wigan coalfield was dominated by several very wealthy and very influential families, none more so than the Lindsays, who had acquired the Haigh Hall estate through marriage and had been mining its coal since the previous century. By the nineteenth century the Lindsay family's commitment to coal mining was absolute, confirmed in a letter from Earl Lindsay to his son, James, in 1822: '. . . our fortune is coal . . . colliers we are, and colliers we must remain.' James was eventually succeeded by his son, Alexander, Earl Balcarres and Earl of Crawford, who would make the Haigh collieries profitable through efficiency measures and acquisitions. By the 1860s the family owned some of the most productive and profitable pits around Wigan. One such operation was the Bawkhouse Colliery, known locally as the Button Pit. Located close to the Lancaster Canal at Red Rock, the Button Pit was a medium-sized concern; extracting coal from the profitable Arley seam, it was no different to countless other similar mines dotted around the town. However, on 3 January 1863, the Button Pit would gain great notoriety when it became the scene of a brutal murder.

Like many mines located on the South Lancashire coalfield,

The Lindsay family, who had acquired the Haigh Hall estate through marriage, were one of the largest mining concerns on the Wigan coalfield, and were the owners of the Button Pit where the murder took place. Although any remains of the Button Pit have long since disappeared, the estate manager's house still stands, bearing the initials EB, standing for the Earl of Balcarres, just one of the titles held by the Lindsay family.

the Button Pit suffered from flooding; water seeped continuously into the mine workings and as a result the pumping engine had to be operated around the clock. The task of ensuring that the engine and its boiler were maintained and stocked with coal fell to a father and son partnership, James and John Barton. John Barton worked the day shift and, after being relieved of his duties by his fifty-eight-year-old father on the night of Friday 2 January, had returned home to their small cottage located not far from the mine. At around 3 am the following morning, James Watmough, a local pony driver, arrived at the mine to feed the animals as he did every morning and almost immediately realised that all was not well. Barton, who would normally greet him every morning and even light a beacon to aid his passage across the moorland, was nowhere to be seen. Despite a quick preliminary search Watmough could not locate him. Barton's son, John, lived in a nearby cottage and so Watmough ran around there and informed John Barton that his father was missing. The two men returned to the mine and, with the aid of lanterns, carried out a more detailed and thorough search of the above-ground workings and outbuildings. Despite the fact that all three of the mine's furnaces

The Crawford Arms at Red Rock was once a hive of activity and a regular haunt for the local mining population, many of whom would have worked at the infamous Button Pit.

were working, their fires were low, and as a result of a drop in pressure in the boiler, the vital pump had stopped working, which suggested that they had not been attended too for several hours. By now the morning shift had arrived at the mine and, although they were concerned for James Barton's welfare, the most important thing was to fire-up the furnace and get the pump working again before they could even consider going underground. John Barton began to shovel coal into the furnaces and soon had the fires high enough for steam to be generated and the pump was working once more. With this he and Watmough continued to look for his father, James. Unable to locate him, and becoming increasingly concerned, the two men contacted the local police.

It took at least a couple of hours before the police arrived, finally reaching the mine just as dawn was breaking. Under daylight conditions, they were able to conduct a much more detailed search of the colliery surface buildings. Although there were fresh bloodstains on several of the walls, and a heavily bloodstained crowbar was found nearby, a close examination of the area still did not yield a body. However, as one of the officers inspected one of the mine's furnaces he made a grim discovery. It would appear that Barton had been struck over the head with a crowbar and bludgeoned to death sometime during the night; then his blood-soaked body was bundled into the furnace in an attempt to incinerate the evidence. The furnaces were allowed to cool so they could be inspected more closely and, with the ashes extracted, the police discovered partially burned bones, along with personal items such as a brass belt buckle.

A murder inquiry was begun. The following day the mine was visited by senior police officers, including Elgee, Lancashire's Chief Constable, along with Earl Lindsay, who immediately issued a sizable reward for information leading to the arrest of James Barton's killer. The distinct lack of motive still puzzled the police and the only reason for Barton's murder that they could determine was robbery, as he carried a distinctive and seemingly valuable silver fob watch and this was now missing. A description of the timepiece was circulated and all of Wigan's dealers in precious metals, pawnbrokers and fences were questioned, but the watch was never seen again. And, despite a thorough investigation, which involved questioning all of his workmates and associates, the police were soon left with no suspects and no leads to act upon. This apparently motiveless crime could not be solved.

By now the incident, referred to as 'The Wigan Murder' in the national press, had attracted interest from far and wide. The inhabitants were eager for news, and yet, although the local press felt duty bound to provide them with a blow by blow account of the case, the police were not being very forthcoming, which resulted in great frustration. For instance, it was reported in the *Wigan Observer* on Friday 23 January that the police had informed the press 'that it might probably prejudice their chances of apprehending the murderers if the whole of the information they possess and the suspicions they hold be made public', a claim which the press described as 'utter nonsense'.

Without any leads to go on, the case began to go cold. The Home Secretary became so concerned that the culprit should be apprehended that he offered a £200 reward and an amnesty to any criminal, even an accomplice in the murder, who came forward to give evidence. Earl Balcarres, owner of the Button Pit and Barton's employer, matched the reward pound for pound – in fact, he would later raise the reward to £500. And yet, despite such inducements no one came forward and with no new evidence. The investigation was scaled down, and eventually shelved.

Strangely enough, some two years later the police would have more suspects than they could handle. The case was reopened after a prisoner held in Warwick Gaol, John Healey, suddenly confessed to the murder of James Barton in Wigan in the January of 1863. Detectives from Wigan police were sent to question Healey and yet even before they had arrived at the jail his spectacular confession had been retracted. Later that same year the case took another unexpected twist when Thomas Walton of Aspull was overheard in a Wigan public house boasting that he knew who had committed what was now known as the 'Button Pit Murder' and even suggested that Barton's silver watch had been discarded by the killer, who had tossed it into the Lancaster Canal from Red Rock Bridge. Wigan police immediately arrested Walton, who claimed that the motive for Barton's murder was not the robbery of his

The section of canal, near Red Rock Bridge, located close to the Button Pit, which was dragged by police following Thomas Walton's bogus claim that the murderer had discarded James Barton's watch there.

valuable watch, but revenge, as he had previously reported the murderer for poaching. However, despite questioning him thoroughly over the allegation he had made a few nights earlier, Walton refused to name the culprits, claiming he was too scared to do so. The police initially took his story seriously and even went to the time and expense of having the Red Rock section of the Leeds & Liverpool Canal dragged, but nothing was found. The police were once again under pressure to find the killer and, believing that Walton, and indeed Healey, knew more about the murder than they were telling both men were charged with having conspired in the murder of James Barton.

However, just when the police thought they were getting somewhere, this peculiar case offered yet another twist. The local press had covered both the 'Healey confession' and the 'Walton boasting' in some detail and had resurrected many of the original crime photographs from two years earlier, including a picture of Barton's silver fob watch. As luck would have it, that picture was seen by a James Grime from Chorley, who recognised it as being one that had previously been in the possession of his brother, Thomas – a notable criminal – who was currently serving a three-year jail term in Dartmoor. However, before beginning his current term of imprisonment Thomas had given his brother, James, a pawn ticket 'for safe keeping'. Sometime later James had redeemed the ticket and, discovering that it was a valuable-looking silver fob watch, sold it to a friend. After reading the recent coverage of the 'Button Pit Murder' in the local press, James Grime had retrieved the watch from his friend and the two men then handed it into the local police station in Chorley.

Detectives from Wigan police station travelled to Chorley and, after first confirming that the watch was indeed the one that had been stolen from James Barton at the time of his murder, interviewed James Grime at length about his wayward brother's activities around 3 January 1863. Satisfied that Thomas Grime was now the prime suspect, Wigan detectives travelled to Dartmoor and conducted an initial interview, on 24 March 1866. Clearly satisfied that Thomas Grime was implicated in the murder of James Barton, the detectives had bought him back to Wigan. Confronted with his brother's statement and the watch as a key piece of damming evidence, Grime confessed being involved in the crime, though he stated that he had not committed the actual murder of James Barton. He told police that there had been two other men present at the mine,

William Thompson and Joseph Seddon, and that it had been Thompson who had struck Barton over the head with the crowbar. However, he later told police that there had actually been another man with them that night, Thomas Walton, who had assisted Thompson in bundling Barton's body into the furnace.

Grime's statement to the police seemed damning, though in actual fact the police were far from convinced. Although a blacksmith by trade, he was a hardened criminal with a noted temper and a liking for violence. Police believed that he was the murderer and Thompson, Seddon, Walton and Healey were his accomplices. Nevertheless, all five suspects were charged with murder. Walton and Healey were tried separately from Grime, Thompson and Seddon. By the time that Walton and Healey appeared in the dock before Justice Mellor at the Liverpool Assizes in April 1866, Healey had a severe case of TB and was very ill. The case against him was weak. Before the court could clear him of all involvement in the murder he died. Walton pleaded not guilty and maintained his innocence throughout the trial. He was, nevertheless, found guilty.

Grime, Thompson and Seddon appeared before Justice Baron Martin at Liverpool Crown Court in August 1866. All three men pleaded not guilty to the charge of murder. Throughout the trial the defence counsel made great play on the fact that there was no evidence to link either of the men to the crime, except handling the watch, and none of them were being charged with 'handling stolen goods'. Seddon, like Healey before him, died of TB before the trial ended. The case against Thompson hinged on the statement which Grime had given to the police and, with no other corroborating evidence to support the accusation, it was one criminal's word against another. Therefore, Thompson was released without charge. Now, with only Grime in the dock, Mr Justice Baron Martin advised the jury that they would have to decide whether he had gone to the mine that night with the intention of murdering Barton, or whether he had gone to 'sort him out'. The judge explained that while the former was 'actual murder', the latter was 'manslaughter'. The jury, enthralled with the trial, did not believe Grime's constant pleas of innocence and, without the need to retire and take time to consider their verdict, found him guilty of the wilful murder of James Barton. When asked did he have anything to say before passing sentence, once more Grime claimed he was innocent, in his words 'as innocent as a child'.

With this, Justice Baron Martin donned his black cap and sentenced him to death.

Later that day, Thomas Walton, who had been found guilty of having participated in the crime, appeared in the dock before Justice Baron Martin. Reviewing the obvious lack of evidence in the case, the judge, realising that Walton's confession to the murder of James Barton had been little more than a drunken boast in a crowded public house, dismissed all charges against him and he walked from the court a free man.

While awaiting his execution at Kirkdale prison, Thomas Grime informed the authorities that he had acted alone in murdering James Barton and, contrary to his earlier statements to the police, neither William Thompson nor Joseph Seddon had anything to do with the crime. And yet, at the same time he was busy telling anyone that would listen to his story, that he was an innocent man. The murder of James Barton at the Button Pit aroused great interest and it seemed only fitting that the execution of Thomas Grime on 1 September 1866 was witnessed by a huge crowd of onlookers.

CHAPTER 3

Feuding Families

1867

Open the door Kitty, and let's see what they want

It's perhaps easy to think that having 'neighbours from hell' is a modern problem, but in actual fact, troublesome neighbours and feuding families have been around for centuries. During the Victorian period, especially in hardy working-class towns like Wigan, feuding families were very common and fights often took place between neighbours. Disputes could begin with the slightest of reason, and then fester in the hearts and minds of the rival families until there was mutual hatred. However, despite arguments, feuds and fights being a seemingly common occurrence, it was much rarer for it to result in a loss of life.

But, there is always the exception to the rule. On Saturday 11 May 1867, retired sailor Patrick Farrell was killed as a direct consequence of a longstanding family feud. It was a confusing case from the outset for the local police to even attempt to fathom. There were more questions than answers. For instance, was Patrick Farrell actually murdered, and if so, then by what means? In fact, what was the murder weapon? Conflicting accounts from so-called eyewitnesses, and with much malice on their part, only helped to further muddy the already murky waters.

Patrick Farrell had retired from the Royal Navy in 1856, and lived with his wife in a little cottage, a humble dwelling, within Moss's Yard, just off Queen Street in the town centre of Wigan. Their immediate neighbours were the Greens, Nathaniel and Ann, who were relatives of the Fairclough family. By all accounts, the Farrells and the Faircloughs had been at loggerheads for some time. It's not certain just how the dispute had begun, but it dated back to a period in time when all the families were living on Wigan Lane. Differences resulted in violence. Mrs Farrell got into some disagreement with Nathaniel Green and he had lashed out and struck her. She had reported the

Wigan Lane, where the feud between the Farrells and the Faircloughs began.

assault to the authorities and had succeeded in having an injunction taken out against him. However, the injunction, rather than solving the matter, made the situation even worse.

Apart from the Greens, other families had been forced to take sides, including the Hursts who also lived on Wigan Lane. They decided to back up the Faircloughs. Matters escalated, and soon there was real hatred between the two warring parties. Even when the Farrells had vacated their home on Wigan Lane for a cottage in Moss's Yard, the trouble continued.

On Saturday 11 May, Patrick Farrell was at home. His wife, Kitty, had been out shopping and had returned home just after 10 pm. Their son, John, who lived in Aspull, had come around for his supper just before 11 pm. A few minutes before, Peter Fairclough and Thomas Hurst, both local colliers at Rose Bridge Colliery, and their wives, came around to Moss's Yard looking for trouble. They went to the home of Nathaniel Green and his wife, Ann (Fairclough's niece, later described in the *Wigan Observer* as being a 'woman of loose character'), before the group gathered outside of the Farrells' cottage. They began causing a disturbance, shouting abuse and banging on Farrell's door, calling for him to come out. Deeply concerned at what might occur if she let them in, Mrs Farrell took the precaution of bolting the door. Repeatedly, they called for Farrell to come outside and when he did not they continued to bang on the door and windows. Despite Kitty pleading with her husband to ignore them, Mr Farrell insisted that he was not going to hide behind any locked door. Unbolting it, he opened the door to see what Fairclough and his companion wanted.

While her husband argued on the front, Mrs Farrell and her son, John, went into the backyard to get away from the disturbance. The argument went on for some time, until suddenly there was a loud bang or thud and Patrick Farrell slumped to the floor, apparently unconscious. Kitty ran to her husband and, finding him 'out cold' thought he was dead and began accusing Fairclough of murder. This infuriated Fairclough and his associates began breaking her windows. The Farrells' son, John, ran out of the yard and summoned the police. P C Atkinson soon arrived on the scene, along with a doctor. Patrick Farrell, still alive, was rushed to Wigan Infirmary. In the meantime, the angry crowd had all gone into the Greens' cottage. When PC Atkinson went inside he discovered that Nathaniel Green had gone, though he was able to arrest both Fairclough and Hurst for the assault on Patrick Farrell and personally escort them to King Street police station, for questioning.

The circumstances behind what had actually happened to Patrick Farrell that evening remain a matter for conjecture. Many of the people concerned would later tell the police that Fairclough had pulled out a gun from inside his jacket and shot Farrell once in the head. Indeed, all of the witnesses confirmed that they had heard a loud bang or thud, and everyone concerned agreed that it had been the report of a firearm which they had heard. However, when the doctors at Wigan Infirmary examined Mr Farrell they found a contusion to the head that was most certainly not as the result of any gunshot, but more likely the result of a blow from a blunt instrument.

Having arrested both Fairclough and Hurst, the police searched Green's home for what they themselves were describing as the 'murder weapon' – even though at this point in time Farrell was still alive and, with the circumstances surrounding the incident being so vague, it was not certain that the intention had been to murder him. It was during a thorough search of the property that police discovered what appeared to be a home-made pistol, less than skilfully hidden inside the chimney breast. This impromptu firearm, later described in court as being a pistol 'formed by a handle of wire rope, a little

Wigan Infirmary, where Patrick Farrell was rushed after sustaining an injury to the head. However, despite the best efforts of the doctors and the nursing staff, Patrick Farrell died on Tuesday 14 May 1867.

Today, Queen Street is almost filled with small industrial units and only a few houses still stand. Moss's Yard has long since been demolished and the only houses located off Queen Street today are the few located in Hartley Terrace, which once stood back-to-back with cottages in Moss's Yard.

over a foot long and wrapped in spun yarn, and a hammer head of two pieces of iron bolted together' was taken to the police station for forensic examination. The discovery of 'the murder weapon' in Green's home and his sudden disappearance from the crime scene caused the police to issue a warrant for his immediate arrest.

Although the police were anxious to speak to Patrick Farrell about the circumstances surrounding the assault, his fragile state was such that he was drifting between consciousness and unconsciousness. His condition got even worse and by the following evening he had slipped into a coma from which he did not recover.

The next morning, Monday 13 May, Fairclough and Hurst appeared at the Moot Court before the Mayor and a local magistrate, Mr T Wall, where they were formally charged with the attempted murder of Patrick Farrell. Chief Constable Simm informed the court that the home-made weapon, which he described as being 'crude but effective', had, in his opinion, only one purpose – to kill. By now forensic examination had shown that there was a wet and sticky deposit on one end, though at this stage they could not confirm categorically that it was blood. The court was informed that Mr Farrell's condition was worsening and, in the doctor's opinion, it was highly unlikely that he would regain consciousness. As the police required more time to conduct more inquiries, and that the makeshift weapon was to be sent to the laboratory in Liverpool for more detailed examination of the wet deposit, the court was adjourned and Fairclough and Hurst remained in custody for another week.

Patrick Farrell's condition took a turn for the worse during the night, and he died on the morning of Tuesday 14 May. This was now officially a murder inquiry. Fairclough and Hurst made a brief appearance at the magistrates' court on the following Monday, when the charge against them was upgraded to one of wilful murder. The court was also informed that the gun was tested by the Royal Institute Laboratory at Liverpool, showing that there was no blood on it whatsoever – though they also informed the court that in their opinion the weapon had been washed thoroughly immediately after the incident. Tests had also discovered some hairs, not human, but from a dog. The magistrates decided to continue the case once the coroner's inquest had concluded its findings.

The inquest, held at the Town Hall, was brief. Mrs Farrell gave evidence, providing background to the ongoing feud between her family, the Greens, Faircloughs and Hursts, and offered her version of the circumstances surrounding the death of her husband. She also added that Nathaniel Green had not

Fairclough and Hurst were arrested and taken to Wigan police station which once stood on King Street.

only been present during the scuffle with her husband, but had played an active role. Nathaniel Green, who had fled Wigan following the attack on Patrick Farrell, had subsequently been arrested in Wales and bought back to Wigan by PC Atkinson. He was now called to give evidence, and told the court how he had been out drinking with Fairclough earlier that evening when they had encountered Mrs Farrell who had shouted abuse at them.

John Smith, a foreman at the Rose Bridge Colliery where both Fairclough and Hurst worked, also gave evidence and confirmed that the men had manufactured the gun from obsolete parts they had scrounged from the mine. Having heard from all concerned, the inquest concluded that Patrick Farrell had died as a result of a blow to the head by a heavy, blunt, metallic object. It also reached the conclusion that Hurst had played little part in the encounter, apart from shouting and banging on the windows and door, though it found that both Fairclough and Hurst were responsible for Patrick Farrell's death.

The matter was now transferred back to the Moot Court, which briefly convened on Thursday 30 May, referring the case on to the Liverpool Assizes on 23 August. There both men were charged with the wilful murder of Patrick Farrell, and both pleaded not guilty. The prosecution was led by Mr Fitzadam and the defence by Mr Pope and Mr Scott. Even before the trial could get under way, legal arguments were put before the judge to reason that both men ought to be tried separately. The judge agreed, and it was Nathaniel Green that would appear first in the dock. The evidence against Green had come from Mrs Farrell's testimony at the coroner's inquest. She had said that it was Green that had acted as a catalyst, stirring up the situation outside their cottage, shouting abuse and, after Patrick Farrell lay unconscious on the floor, he had been the one who had broken her windows. And the murder weapon had been discovered in his cottage during the police search. However, in

Fairclough and Hurst appeared at the Borough Court on Monday 13 May, before the Mayor and a local magistrate, Mr T Wall, where they were formally charged with the attempted murder of Patrick Farrell.

Green's favour, the matter was very vague and the evidence against him weak. Therefore, the judge would advise the jury that to convict Green of murder they would have to believe beyond reasonable doubt that he was the one that had inflicted the fatal blow. Responding to the judge's direction, the jury reached their decision without the need to retire, finding Nathaniel Green not guilty of murder. With no case to answer, Nathanial Green walked free from the court.

Peter Fairclough had his turn in the dock the following day, 24 August. The prosecution, led by Mr Fitzadam, did their best to implicate Fairclough in the murder, though in actual fact there was less evidence against him than there had been against Nathaniel Green, who had been acquitted by a jury just the day before. The defence, led by Mr Pope and Mr Scott, played on the fact that all of the so-called 'damning evidence' against their client, and indeed the same evidence that had been discredited against Nathaniel Green, had come solely from the testimony of Kitty Farrell. The defence counsel suggested that much of what Mrs Farrell had said was less than truthful and, as the court had already heard of the hatred between the two families, that her account of the events on the evening in question was spiteful and malicious. Without Mrs Farrells' testimony there was no one else that could say what had happened exactly outside the Farrell's cottage that night, not least who indeed had struck Mr Farrell over the head. Once again, the judge felt the need to advise the jury, telling them that to find Peter Fairclough guilty of murder they would have to be convinced that he was the man that had inflicted the fatal blow. Having heard all the available evidence, the jury concluded that there was insufficient evidence to convict Fairclough of murder and therefore found him not guilty. Interestingly, Ann Green, the woman of 'loose character', was also charged with the murder of Farrell, but this was later thrown out by the jury.

CHAPTER 4

A Scalded Child

1868

. . . this particular child always screamed when it was being washed, though . . . on this occasion, it screamed all the more

Wigan was the first town in Lancashire to open a House of Correction. The institute had been established in 1608 under the rules of the Elizabethan Poor Law, and although its primary purpose was to act as a prison, its secondary, though equally important role was to take care of the poor, sick, elderly and destitute. However, in spite of its initial success, the House of Correction would be forced to close within a decade due mainly to financial constraints, and a new, larger facility was opened at Preston in 1617. By the following century, the need to support the most vulnerable members of society led to the opening of a number of small parish workhouses. In Wigan the main institution held a maximum of 200 inmates, while outside the town districts, such as Dalton, Pemberton and Standish, each had their own workhouse, with a much smaller capacity, normally housing around forty inmates.

The administration of the poor changed dramatically following the passing of the 1834 Poor Law Amendment Act, which established Poor Law Unions throughout the country, each controlled by a Board of Guardians. These worthies, locally elected officials, together with at least one Justice of the Peace, held their position for life – though it was not unusual for some of them to fail to carry out their duties.

However, these new measures, which attempted to make poor relief more uniform in its administration, were slow to be implemented, and Wigan's Poor Law Union was not established until 2 February 1837. The new administration, controlled by a board of twenty guardians, was now responsible not just for Wigan but a further nineteen parishes, with a combined population of 58,402. As time went by, and particularly as the population continued to increase and showed no signs of slowing, the constraints on the old parish workhouses became too much and the Board of Guardians commissioned architect William Mangnall to built a new, larger workhouse on land off Frog Lane. Work commenced in 1855 and the institution was operational two years later.

Life in the Union workhouses was harsh. Destitute families were taken into there, and once within its walls, parents would be separated from their children, and husbands segregated from their wives. Although the funds available ought to have provided more than adequate food for the residents, more often than not inmates' rations were meagre. Many children were born in the workhouse and, despite medical supervision, many would end their days there too.

The number of staff within the workhouse was limited, in fact many of the 'staff' were inmates themselves. In a system rather like a 'prison trustee', inmates were encouraged to actively participate in the day-to-day duties of the regime, and those who

The Frog Lane Union Workhouse, which had opened its doors in 1857, was a terrible place (and most Wiganers would have considered it a 'fate worse than death') and a harsh environment in which to live. Following its closure in 1970 (then known as Frog Lane Hospital) the building was demolished, and today only a section of the perimeter wall remains.

could show merit were awarded certain daily duties, paid for with increased food rations. Much of the work was barely supervised, and many accidents occurred. The horrific and needless death of Ruth Bannister, a five-year-old workhouse-born infant, is a case in point.

Ruth died on Monday 6 January 1868, after being placed into a bucket of boiling water by Catherine Dawber, a seventeen-year-old 'nurse' on the infant ward. A coroner's inquest was held on Wednesday 15 January to enquire into the circumstances that had conspired to cause the death of the infant. The Borough Coroner, Ralph Darlington, presided, aided by Mr Ackersley, clerk to the Board of Guardians.

The first witness to be called was fellow workhouse inmate, Cicely O'Conner who had previously lived at Griffin Yard. She had been in the Wigan workhouse for just over two months, though she pointed out that her husband had been there for nine months, since he lost his job. Cicely informed the court that on Monday 6 January, she had been washing clothes in the cook house, and at around 9 am Catherine Dawber had come in to fill a bucket with water directly from the boiler. Because there was no tap on the boiler water had to be ladled directly out from the top, and this was strictly against the rules. Cicely added that the matron, Mrs Swallow, had told everyone concerned, on several previous occasions, not to do such a thing. Cicely O'Conner informed the coroner that she had told Catherine Dawber not to do this, but she had replied: 'If you would give me two quarts, I would not come again.' O'Conner told her to hurry, before the matron could come in and catch them.

At this point, the coroner interrupted, enquiring: 'So a junior had been in the habit of fetching water?'

'No, sir,' replied O'Conner, before adding: 'Catherine Dawber did not say what she wanted the water for, sir, and I did not know where she took it.'

Cicely O'Conner was dismissed and the next witness to take the stand was Margaret Gaskell, a workhouse supervisor, who gave evidence regarding the everyday running of the institution. When asked about the competence of Catherine Dawber, Mrs Gaskell referred to her as being 'an imbecile'. This statement caused some confusion, as Mr Darlington enquired as to whether the institution actually recognised Catherine Dawber as being an 'imbecile' in the true meaning of the term, i.e. someone with far less than normal mental understanding. Mrs

Gaskell replied that she did not know for certain. Later, when further enquiries were made into the workhouse records, it was discovered that Catherine Dawber, though slow and sometimes awkward in her manner, was not officially classified as being an imbecile.

This confusion aside, a much clearer picture of the circumstances surrounding Ruth Bannister's peculiar death was gained when the seventy-three-year-old Ann Hart gave her evidence. Hart had lived in the workhouse for much of her life and had been working on the infant ward for some considerable time. Hart told the court that it was while Catherine Dawber was washing the child that she placed the infant into the bucket of what turned out to be scalding water, but added, 'only for a minute'. She went on to say that although she was on the ward that morning and had seen Dawber place the child into the water, she was not close by and had not known that the water had been taken directly from the boiler in the cook house. She also explained that it was normal practice, when bathing the infants, to take warm water from one of two taps near the infant ward. Ann Hart then informed the court that she herself had bathed hundreds of infants and, although she only had the use of one of her arms, nothing like this had ever happened to her. When asked by the coroner: 'Didn't the child scream?' Hart explained that: 'This particular child always screamed when it was being washed, though, I have to say that, on this occasion, it screamed all the more.' Hart then described what happened next: 'Dawber took the child out of the bucket and laid it upon her knee, and as soon as she commenced rubbing I saw the skin peel off and I stopped her.'

William Raynor, the workhouse surgeon and deputy to Mr Winstanley, medical officer of the workhouse, was also called to give evidence. He told the court that he made his usual visit on the day in question and when he reached the infant ward had discovered the infant, Ruth Bannister, dead on the nurse's knee. He told the court that 'the infant was scalded on both legs, up to about two inches above the knee, and the skin was hanging in shreds'. Death, in his opinion, had been caused by 'a shock to the system, and the severe scalding had also caused inflammation of the lungs'. He concluded his evidence by confirming that the infant had been born in Wigan's Union workhouse, and during all previous medical examinations he had found her to be in 'perfect health and very well nourished'.

The court was also informed that Catherine Dawber had

herself been scalded on a previous occasion, when she was about twelve years old, and the severe scarring to her neck had impeded her speech and often made her difficult to understand.

Having heard all the evidence, the coroner summed up the case, referring to the circumstances as 'most bizarre' and expressed his disbelief at the circumstances surrounding the cruel death of Ruth Bannister. He went on to say that Catherine Dawber must have been aware of just how hot the water was, as she had taken it directly from the boiler. Equally, it is almost impossible to believe that at no time had her hand not come in contact with the scalding water, either before or during the time she was bathing the infant. He concluded that he did not believe that Catherine Dawber had had any intention of harming the infant, intentionally or otherwise. He advised the jury that 'in my opinion, there was no evidence showing that any act of absolute wilfulness, but if the jury were of a contrary opinion it would be their duty to return a verdict of wilful murder, between which and one of accidental death there does not appear to be any middle course'.

The jury retired to consider their verdict. After deliberating for only an hour-and-a-half they returned to the court room and delivered their verdict. Finding Catherine Dawber guilty of manslaughter, the foreman made the following statement: 'The deceased died in consequence of being negligently and carelessly scalded whilst being cared for by Catherine Dawber.' He also passed comment on the state of the infant ward saying: 'The nursing in the infant ward is very deficient and most unsatisfactory,' and added 'there ought to be a responsible person in charge of the ward.'

The horrors of this clear case of neglect not only caused an outrage in late-Victorian Wigan, causing Mr and Mrs Swallow, master and matron of the workhouse, to resign, but led to an inquiry into the practices of Wigan's Union workhouse. Basil Caine, the Poor Law Inspector, visited the Frog Lane institution on Wednesday 23 February to witness for himself the scene of the 'horrific accident' and to conduct a detailed inspection of the facilities available for inmates. His subsequent report was wide-ranging and covered more than just good practice and safety, but also the quality of the food the inmates ate and their overall standard of living. As a result, life for the inmates of Wigan's Union workhouse improved significantly.

CHAPTER 5

Kicked to Death

1868

God forgive thee . . . tha's murdered me

Domestic violence is nothing new. Couples have been rowing and fighting for centuries, and the distinct increase in the number of public houses in Victorian working-class towns like Wigan, and cheaply priced beer, conspired to make the situation far worse. The Jacksons were a typical case in point, as John had fought with his wife, Mary, on many occasions, often when one or both of them had been drinking. However, on Tuesday 2 June 1868, matters went too far when, following a heavy drinking session, Jackson returned home drunk and, provoked by a flippant remark from his wife, kicked her to death.

John Jackson was thirty-two and had worked at the Kirkless Hall Works, owned by the Wigan Coal & Iron Company, as a boiler maker, for several years. He lived with his wife, Mary, in a small house at Caldwell Fold, Birkett Bank, near Scholes, on the outskirts of Wigan town centre. Theirs could not be described as a happy or content marriage, as the couple often argued, and these disagreements often led to violence. Matters were exacerbated by drink and both of them were heavy imbibers, frequently visiting hostelries in and around Wigan.

It was an uneasy union. Broadly considered to be both amusing and annoying by their neighbours, the Jacksons' squabbles and fights often reached such a pitch that the police had been called to break them up. On several occasions they appeared in court and were bound over to keep the peace. Mr Jackson was a large, burly man who could certainly handle himself, but Mrs Jackson was no shrinking violet when it came to fighting, as she had attacked her husband on several occasions, often when intoxicated. Matters reached such a point where John Jackson preferred charges against her for assault. Mary Jackson had been imprisoned twice, and on release had once again been bound over to keep the peace.

The Jacksons had had one of their now legendary rows about two weeks prior to the night of the murder. Mr Jackson had thrown his wife out of the house and forced her to live rough for almost ten days. Caldwell Fold consisted of just two rows of basic two-up, two-down terraced houses, and in between the rows was a basic wooden shed, referred to locally as 'the closet'. It was in this humble abode that Mrs Jackson had been sleeping rough for the week or so during the period in which her husband had forbid her to return to the marital home. She had existed simply on the goodwill and charity of her neighbours, who were fearful of actually taking her into their homes and putting a secure roof over her head, and yet at the same time felt that they could not simply sit back and watch the poor woman go without. They brought her food on a daily basis and allowed her to bathe and wash her clothes.

On Sunday 31 May, John Jackson reconciled his differences with his wife and allowed her back into the family home. Delighted and relieved to be home again, Mary Jackson busied herself cleaning and tidying her little property which had been neglected for the period of her banishment. On the day in question, Tuesday 2 June, Mary had been home all day, spending her time washing and cleaning while her husband was at work.

On that particular day, however, John Jackson was late, arriving home at 10 pm. He had departed work at the usual time but, rather than coming straight home for his evening meal with his wife, spent the evening drinking in the public houses. By the time he got home he was heavily intoxicated. He staggered up to the door and banged on it loudly, but there was no answer. He banged again, but still there was no answer. He even shouted his wife's name through the letter box but once again there was no response. Infuriated, he reluctantly walked away.

Within minutes he was back. By now his wife had appeared and was leaning against the garden wall. Jackson was far from pleased and, as she handed him the front door key, he said to her: 'Where's tha been, tha little nasty **** . . .' Mary replied, in a very sarcastic tone, that she had been where he had been, drinking in the *White Swan* (a noted hostelry at Scholes). This was like a red rag to a bull, and John Jackson came towards his wife in an aggressive manner. Realising that she had perhaps said too much and she was now in for a beating, Mary Jackson retreated, going along the gable end of the house. John followed, and an argument ensued.

Although some terraced houses still exist at Birkett Bank today, massive redevelopment through the years means that Caldwell Fold, where the Jacksons lived, has long since disappeared.

By now, the noise of the argument had brought several of the Jacksons' neighbours out on to their fronts to witness yet another aggressive display from the neighbourhood's 'rowing couple'. Watching Mr Jackson pursuing his wife to the rear of their house in an aggressive manner, some of the neighbours, fearing violence was about to break out, quickly followed them. They arrived at the rear of the terraced row in time to witness

Mrs Jackson lying on the floor and Mr Jackson repeatedly kicking her. Despite the fact that Mrs Jackson had rolled herself up in a tight ball in an effort to protect herself, this did not prevent her husband kicking her in the head and torso with brutal force. Seeing the neighbours standing there watching him caused Jackson to end the violent onslaught. This pause gave Mary the opportunity to scream at the assembled crowd of onlookers: 'He's killed me!' and then, turning to look up at her husband towering above her, she said: 'God forgive thee . . . tha's murdered me.'

With this, several of the neighbours ran to fetch the police. John Jackson in the meantime walked away from his wife, back towards his house, though not before cursing his neighbours for their unwanted interference, and threatening them as to what they might expect from him, with the boasting phrase: 'I'm capable of fighting any **** man in Wigan.' Meanwhile, Mary, who had been laying still on the ground after the intense beating, now began to painfully crawl along the rough ground, attempting to take refuge in the closet were she had previously spent so many nights. Although she reached it, she was badly injured, blood pouring from a severe cut to her head. She managed to sit upright momentarily before slumping forward with her head in her lap; but never moved again after. She was dead.

PC O'Brien arrived on the scene soon afterwards. Walking over to Mary Jackson's crumpled body, slumped in the tiny shed, he confirmed that she was in fact deceased. Having gained an account of the evening's events from the assembled neighbours, PC O'Brien arrested John Jackson on the suspicion of his wife's murder and took him to the local police station. The constable later returned to the murder scene accompanied by Mr Heaton the police surgeon, and a few minutes later another surgeon, Mr Monks, also arrived. Inspecting the scene, they saw a large pool of blood where the deceased had laid.

When questioned at the police station, John Jackson told officers: 'I never struck her. I never touched her, or kicked her, in any form or shape whatsoever.' He was held in custody and appeared before the Mayor and Mr J Lamb, a local magistrate, in the Moot Court on 31 May, where he was formally charged with 'killing his wife by kicking her in the abdomen'. The Chief Constable informed the court of the couple's turbulent marriage, and of their previous rows and fights. Although he informed the court that the Jacksons were well known to the police, the Chief Constable added that 'of late they had settled down again at Caldwell Fold'. A neighbour, Mary Burrows, also gave evidence. She told the court that on the night in question John Jackson had passed her in the street before scolding the deceased and attacking her without provocation.

Mr Darlington, the Borough Coroner, convened an inquest on Thursday afternoon at the *Raven Inn*. The prisoner was represented by Mr Ashton, a local solicitor. The Jacksons' eldest son, Joseph, who had left home some eight years earlier, was called as a witness, and told the court how he knew that both his parents were fond of drink. He also added that he had been informed of his mother's death that same evening and when he came around to the family home he found the police and the surgeon already there.

The inquest was adjourned until the morning of Monday 7 June, when it was resumed in the Grand Jury room of the Borough Offices. In the meantime, Dr Charles Shepherd conducted a port-mortem examination on Mrs Jackson's body, and informed the court that she had died from a 'loss of blood from a laceration wound about one and a half inches long and three quarter inches deep in the upper part of the vagina'. When asked by the coroner: 'What could have caused such a wound?' he replied: 'It was from an outside force, such as would have been produced by a kick.' Dr Shepherd also added that during the course of his examination he had discovered that Mrs Jackson had been suffering from a disease of the heart. But when he was asked by the Chief Constable: 'Would this have caused her death?' he replied: 'No. I think that it would not have materially shortened her life.'

Several neighbours were called to offer an account of the events of the evening in question. These included Mary Burrows, who had spoken at the coroner's inquest. Another witness, George Carter, who lived just a few doors away from the Jacksons, said that he had seen the prisoner arrive home. Carter gave an account of what he had seen that evening, saying that the prisoner had struck the deceased, knocked her over the wall, before pursing her to the rear of the property where he and other witnesses had seen him kick her repeatedly.

Having heard all of the evidence, the jury's decision to return a verdict of manslaughter surprised many, including the Chief Constable, Mr Simm, who took the case before the Borough Magistrates' Court on Wednesday 10 June in an attempt to get the decision upgraded to murder. Several witnesses were called and, having heard all of the evidence, the magistrates concurred with Mr Simm and committed Jackson to stand trial for murder at the forthcoming assizes.

Jackson appeared before Justice Baron Martin at the Liverpool Assizes on Thursday 13 August, where he pleaded not guilty to the charge of wilful murder of his wife, Mary Jackson. The prosecution counsel, led by Mr Stott, attempted to portray John Jackson as an evil and violent thug who, on the evening in question, had brutally attacked his wife without provocation. The defence counsel, led by Mr Pope, attempted to claim that their client had not inflicted the fatal wound to the deceased's groin, suggesting that she could easily have injured herself while climbing over the garden wall. The jury clearly did not accept such a claim, though neither did they fully believe the prosecution's case, as they found Jackson guilty of manslaughter. While sentencing him to fourteen years' penal servitude, the judge referred to the case as 'one of a very aggravated character'.

CHAPTER 6

The Ackhurst Hall Murder

1868

They've killed my children!

Gathurst is a quiet rural location on the outskirts of Wigan. Located on the Orrell coalfield, Gathurst gained importance with the opening of the Douglas Navigation and later with the opening of the Leeds & Liverpool Canal. However, the hamlet became a popular retreat with many merchants from both Manchester and Wigan following the construction of the Manchester & Southport Railway in 1855 and the opening of a small station. There are many old halls within this area, such as Ackhurst Hall, which stands on the hillside above Gathurst and the Douglas Valley, constructed from local stone during the Tudor period.

In 1868, Ackhurst Hall, situated in farmland at the bottom of Ackhurst Lane, was owned by the Roper family. Joseph Roper was a wealthy Wigan merchant and entrepreneur, who owned a number of collieries on the Orrell coalfield. Located further along the lane, though close to the old hall, was a converted barn where the Houghton family lived. Mr Houghton had been in the employ of Mr Roper for many years, initially as a clerk, though more recently as the farm and estate manager. He was a trusted and valued employee whom Roper respected. Mr and Mrs Houghton, their five daughters and two sons, enjoyed living in this idyllic setting until an incident which occurred on Tuesday 15 December 1868.

Mr Roper had been to Manchester on business. William Houghton and his wife had gone down to Gathurst station to meet his train which was due at 6.30 pm, leaving his two daughters alone in the house. Roper's train was on time that evening and the Houghtons accompanied him to Ackhurst Hall. Although they were invited inside they only stayed for a little while before beginning the short walk home. As they made their way along the narrow track that led to Ackhurst Lane and their house they met Thomas Parkinson, Roper's colliery under-

In 1868, Ackhurst Hall was the home of Joseph Roper, a wealthy Wigan merchant and entrepreneur, who owned a number of collieries on the Orrell coalfield.

manager. The two men chatted as they made their way towards the house.

Mrs Houghton was slightly ahead of the rest and, glancing across the field through the twilight, she could see 'a white substance lying on the grass'. At first she thought it was perhaps a flock of ducks. Clambering over the fence, she made her way across the field for a closer inspection. It was then that she realised that it was a girl's body. As she crouched beside it, she was soon horrified to discover that it was their eldest daughter, Annie. She had been severely beaten about the head and torso and was lying in a pool of blood. Her clothes were later described as being 'plentifully splattered' with blood.

Mrs Houghton screamed: 'They've killed my children.' Mr Houghton and Mr Parkinson came running; in fact even the Ropers were alarmed by the scream and came out of the Hall to see what the commotion was. Meanwhile, Mrs Houghton ran to the house and, finding the door wide open, dashed inside, shouting for her youngest daughter Kate, though there was no reply. The sight that met her when she entered the kitchen must

Gathurst railway station, where William Houghton and his wife had gone to meet Mr Roper's train on the evening of Tuesday 15 December, leaving his two daughters alone in the house.

have sent a shiver down her spine and a stake through her heart, as the walls, the floor and the table were splattered with blood. Frantic, she ran outside, still screaming her daughter's name at the top of her voice. Just when she was beginning to think that Kate had also been murdered, out of the darkness came a little voice, which answered her screams. It was Kate, who had been hiding from her attacker.

By now Mrs Houghton had been joined in the house by her distraught husband, along with Thomas Parkinson and Mr and Mrs Roper. Mr Roper sent word to summon the police from the station at Pemberton and, while they waited for them to arrive, a tearful and terrified Kate, who had now been carried back inside the house, began to relate the events that had occurred earlier that evening. She said that both she and her sister had remained in the house when their parents had left to meet Mr Roper's train, and reassured her father in particular that the door had remained locked. However, at about 7 pm, Annie had noticed that the fire was fading and had unlocked the door and gone out into the yard to fetch a shovelful of coal. As she returned a man had suddenly appeared behind her in the

Ackhurst Lane, the route used by the Houghtons and Mr Roper as they unsuspectingly walked up to the Hall that December evening . . .

open doorway, startling both of the girls. He had asked was this the residence of William Houghton? Annie had told him that, yes it was, but her father was out at the moment attending to business with Mr Roper up at Ackhurst Hall. It was when she had told him this that the man became enraged and had pulled out a large hammer from inside his jacket and, before Annie had had the opportunity to react, had struck her over the head. Kate explained that the initial blow, although severe, had not rendered Annie unconscious, and she had attempted to run away from him, but the man had pursued her into the kitchen where he had struck her again with the hammer on several occasions. Despite this, Annie had managed to get by her attacker and run out of the door and into the darkness, doubt-less trying to make her way to Ackhurst Hall to raise the alarm. The man ran after her and struck her about the head yet again, this time delivering the fatal blow.

With Annie dead, the assailant had come back into the house and proceeded to attack Kate. Striking her on the back of the head and the upper body with the hammer, he then snatched her around the throat before throwing her to the floor and stamping and kicking her. All the time the man was attacking

Kate he was ranting and cursing, referring to the police as 'devils' and threatening that he would kill her and the baby which was in the cradle in the kitchen. In the end he picked up Kate by the throat and threw her out of the door and into the field, leaving her lying on the ground, battered and bleeding.

The man now went back inside and proceeded to ransack the house. He threw his heavily bloodstained hammer on top of the dresser, where it left a tell-tale stain and began pulling out drawers, in search of valuables. And yet, despite his best efforts, the family would later discover that the only item that was missing was a silver fob watch.

The police were summoned by Joseph Roper and the first on the scene was Superintendent Ellison of Pemberton police

Despite extensive modernisation, the former barn where the Houghton family once lived, and the scene of a brutal murder on 15 December 1868, still bears the name 'Houghtons Barn' to this day.

station, followed soon after by Dr Huet, a surgeon from Up Holland. Although Superintendent Ellison would be in overall charge of the murder inquiry, the investigation was headed by Inspector Barker of Standish police station. Matters were made more complicated by the location of the murder, on the border between north and south Lancashire, and so Superintendent Ellison confirmed that he would liaise with his counterpart at Chorley police headquarters.

At daybreak the investigation got under way with Sergeant Bennet leading a number of constables in a detailed search of the surrounding farmland. It wasn't long before they discovered the murder weapon, a large lump hammer, in a wheat field around 100 yards from the house, clearly discarded by the attacker as he made good his escape. Mr Parkinson, Mr Roper's colliery manager, was summoned and easily identified it as one left in the smithy around 5.30 pm. He told police that he was certain that it was the same hammer as it had a partially broken shaft.

The police soon came to the conclusion that the motive behind such a callous attack had been robbery. It was common knowledge locally that William Houghton, in his role as farm and estate manager, also acted as the wages clerk and often kept sizable amounts of cash on the premises. Mr Roper, Houghton's employer, was horrified that an innocent young girl had been murdered by a robber in pursuit of his cash, and immediately put up a reward of £50 for information leading to the murderer's arrest. The murder was given a great deal of coverage, in both the local and national press. Such a horrific murder had come to the attention of the Home Secretary, who matched the reward offered by Houghton's employer, Mr Roper.

The savagery of the murder sent a shock wave throughout the area. It was a crime unheard of in a quiet rural location such as Gathurst, a sentiment conveyed by the *Wigan Observer* on Friday 18 December, when it opened its coverage of the attack with the words: 'Happily crimes of the most serious magnitude are in this district few in number and of rare occurrence . . .'

Annie Houghton was buried in the graveyard of the family church, St James at Orrell, on 20 December. Ten days later, the deputy coroner, Mr C E Driffield, convened an inquest into the murder at the *Springs Inn* at Orrell. Along with Superintendent Ellison, Colonel Bruce, Chief Constable for the County of Lancashire, also made an appearance. Nine-year-old Kate

Annie Houghton was buried in the graveyard of the family church, St James at Orrell, on 20 December 1868.

Houghton, the only surviving witness to the murder, was the first to give evidence and told the court the harrowing details of what had happened to her and her sister on the evening of 15 December. She also confirmed that the hammer, which the police had discovered in the field on the following morning 'was like the one used'. Thomas Parkinson, apart from confirming that the hammer was one of several used in the colliery smithy, also said that when they had discovered the body of Annie Houghton she was already 'quite cold'.

The inquest proved to be very distressing for Mr and Mrs Houghton. For, apart from having to listen to their daughter, Kate, describing the events and the circumstances surrounding their eldest daughter's murder, they also heard the evidence provided by Dr Hurst, the police surgeon who had carried out the autopsy. He confirmed that the girl had died as a result of massive trauma to the brain as the direct result of a heavy blow to the skull by the murder weapon. Dr Hurst went on to say that the hammer had smashed Annie's head with such force as to drive pieces of her skull and hair deep into her brain. He told the coroner that as a result of such a massive blow death would have been instantaneous.

At the end of the inquest, the coroner concluded that Annie Houghton had been wilfully murdered by an unknown assailant and that police inquiries were ongoing. It was a great surprise to all concerned that within eight days a man was arrested and charged with the wilful murder of Annie Houghton. Thomas Jones, a local collier, had been seen acting suspiciously around some railway sidings at Brighouse and had been arrested by PC Strange of the West Riding Constabulary. Aware of the 'Gathurst Murder', when Superintendent Hornby realised that Jones was a collier and from the Wigan area, he contacted his counterpart in the Wigan Constabulary, Superintendent Ellison. Ellison sent Inspector Dickinson over to question Jones on 30 December and, satisfied that he could help them with their enquiries, he was brought back to Wigan for further questioning. Jones was formally charged with the murder of Annie Houghton on 2 January 1869.

When Thomas Jones appeared in court the police felt that he was their man and that they had massed a great deal of evidence against him. In reality, however, they could not have been more wrong. The prosecution's case began to unravel almost from the start, when they had to admit that Kate Houghton, their only witness, had been unable to identify Thomas Jones as the man who had attacked her and murdered her sister. Nevertheless, the prosecution had other evidence. Jones had been lodging at a house owned by John Dickinson in Haydock, a coal mining village located between Wigan and St Helens, around the time of the murder. When he left for Halifax, Dickinson had described the clothes Thomas Jones had been wearing, including a pair of stained trousers. During the time he was in Yorkshire, Jones had sold this pair of trousers, though they had since been recovered by police and were found to have bloodstains on them. The prosecution now claimed that the blood belonged to Annie Houghton, and that the trousers had been splattered with her blood during the murder. However, when challenged about these stains, Jones had said that he had purchased the trousers second-hand and the stains had been on them at the time of the purchase. To the prosecution's immense embarrassment, further inquires revealed that Jones had been telling the truth, as his story was corroborated by the shopkeeper. Further testimony from John Dickinson, Jones's former landlord, provided Jones with a cast-iron alibi. He told the court that Thomas Jones had been working at the Garswood Hall Colliery on the day of the murder and, finishing his shift at midday, he had returned to his lodgings where he remained throughout the evening, retiring to bed at 8 pm.

With Thomas Jones acquitted, the police had no other suspect for the murder of Annie Houghton and, in spite of the sizable reward, no one ever came forward to help with their enquiries. The case remains unsolved.

CHAPTER 7

The Moss Brook Farm Incident

1869

Could the victim have recovered from such a severe beating?

U p Holland was once a rural location, a tiny village gathered around the priory church, surrounded by green fields and moors. Dig Moor once stretched to the west, its attractive landscape of rich and fertile farmland visible as far as the eye could see. Today the scene has changed dramatically, largely built on by the ever-expanding Skelmersdale new town and its industrial estates. The moor no longer exists, now a sprawling mass of houses and flats. During

Dig Moor once stretched to the west of Up Holland village; however, today the landscape has changed dramatically, largely built on by the ever-expanding Skelmersdale new town and its industrial estates, the Moor no longer exists and is instead a sprawling mass of houses and flats.

the nineteenth century, Dig Moor's fertile agricultural land contained many farms, including Moss Brook, the location of a violent assault in 1869.

Farmer John Brown was a man who liked a drink, even though he knew full well that when intoxicated his foul temper could often get the better of him. Now forty-four years old, he had inherited Moss Brook Farm from his father some years before. He lived there with his wife, two sons and a daughter. Brown was a devoted Methodist who never missed a service at his local chapel. Along with his wife and daughter, he attended a foundation stone-laying ceremony at the Primitive Methodist Chapel, Dig Moor on the day of a murder, Tuesday 27 September 1869.

Brown had left his eldest son, Richard, in charge of the farm while he was away. It was a busy time of year, and the Browns employed a number of men, mainly Irish labourers, who also lodged at the farm. These hands helped to bring in the harvest from the fields.

John Leatherbarrow and Thomas Jardine brought a threshing machine to Moss Brook. With them was a third man, George Ashton, who was known to the Browns. Ashton had previously worked on the farm for some time and had been a good worker, though he was fond of a drink and had been warned for coming to work intoxicated on several previous occasions. Just a week before, Ashton had turned up for work in a drunken state and, when challenged by John Brown, had become very abusive. Brown fired him. Unemployed, Ashton sought work as a labourer with Jardine and Leatherbarrow. Ashton explained the situation to Richard Brown and assured him that there was no hard feeling between him and his father, and that he was just there to assist his employers in setting up the threshing machine to be used for tomorrow's harvesting. Richard accepted his explanation and the men got on with the task of setting up the machine. Later, as Richard was about to leave and go to Up Holland, he asked George Ashton to take the keys around to his father, who by now, as the chapel ceremony had ended, would be drinking in his local, the *Bowling Green Inn,* Dig Moor.

Ashton agreed, and accompanied John Leatherbarrow to the pub where they found John Brown already the worse for drink. Brown was noted for his argumentative and aggressive nature when he had downed a pint or two, and this instance was certainly no exception. He began to quarrel with Ashton, and the argument appeared to be becoming more and more heated, on the verge of turning violent. When Leatherbarrow attempted to intervene and calm the situation, Brown turned on him, challenging him to step outside for a fight. Leatherbarrow's diplomatic skills must have been exceptional, as he managed to calm Brown down, talking him out of fighting. All three men sat down and had a peaceful drink. That 'peaceful drink' worked – but turned into several more. Therefore, when they left the *Bowling Green Inn* much later that evening they were all intoxicated, Brown in a much worse state than the others.

They all walked back to Moss Brook Farm together, with the other two men having to steady Brown to stop him falling over. Regardless of the early aggressive encounter, all three men now seemed to get on well with one another and any onlooker would have imagined that it was three friends walking home after an evening in the local pub. Upon reaching Moss Brook Farm, John Brown invited Ashton and Leatherbarrow to come in for yet another drink. Unlocking the kitchen door with his key, Brown invited them inside and then locked the door, replacing the key in his trouser pocket.

Without any provocation, Brown suddenly became aggressive, picked up a poker from the kitchen grate and struck Leatherbarrow over the head with a heavy blow. Leatherbarrow immediately collapsed to the floor, blood gushing from a deep cut to his forehead. Ashton, clearly fearing that he was going to get some of the same treatment, ran out of the kitchen and hid in the adjacent larder. Although Brown struck Leatherbarrow repeatedly with the poker, the latter somehow managed to fight back and wrestle the weapon from the farmer's grasp. Now, with the farmer disarmed, Leatherbarrow insisted that Brown unlock the kitchen door. At first Brown refused, but when threatened with the poker, he put his hand in his trouser pocket, drew out the key and unlocked the door. Once it was far enough open Leatherbarrow dropped the poker on the kitchen floor and bolted for safety, out in the farmyard. Brown, however, was far from finished, and immediately snatched up the poker and pursued him. Leatherbarrow was chased across the cobbled farmyard, but he was in much better physical shape than the farmer and easily managed to get away. Losing sight of his prey in the darkness, Brown returned to the kitchen, locking the door behind him and went in search of Ashton, who was now hiding somewhere in the house – alone.

Sometime during the early hours of Tuesday morning, John

Brown came outside and, walking around to the farm building where the Irish labourers were sleeping, he woke them and told them to come and help him 'move something'. When they came inside the farmhouse they found George Ashton lying bloody and battered on the floor of the larder. At first the Irishmen thought he was dead, but Brown assured them that he was still alive. As they lifted him off the floor, Ashton regained consciousness, and asked to be taken 'where there was a little straw'. The Irish labourers carried Ashton out to the barn, where they laid him on bales of straw and left him there until later in the morning. When dawn broke over Moss Brook Farm, on Wednesday 28 September Jardine and Leatherbarrow got up for work and found George Ashton still in the barn where they had left him the night before. He was dead, doubtless as a direct result of the dreadful injuries inflicted by Brown during the night.

The police were summoned. PC Chitson from Skelmersdale quickly arrived at the scene. He was shown George Ashton's body, still lying on top of the straw bales in the barn, before he

Arrested on the suspicion of murdering George Ashton by PC Chitson, farmer John Brown was subsequently taken to Ormskirk Police Station by Sergeant Parker for questioning.

On Thursday 29 September, John Brown was brought before the Ormskirk Magistrates' Court and formally charged with the murder of George Ashton.

went to challenge the farmer. John Brown was still in what the constable would later refer to in court as a 'state of intoxication', with fresh bloodstains on his hands and clothes – and incoherent. Unable to extract a satisfactory explanation as to the events of the previous evening, PC Chitson arrested Brown on suspicion of murdering George Ashton.

Brown was taken to Ormskirk police station by Sergeant Parker. When questioned, he explained that two men, Leatherbarrow and Ashton, had got him drunk and, after walking him back to the farm, had attempted to rob him in his own home. Brown told the police that he had had no option but to fight back and had grabbed the poker and wildly lashed out in self-defence. The police were far from convinced, especially as Brown had not reported the incident. Later, after questioning Leatherbarrow on the events of the previous evening, they questioned Brown again. Challenging his earlier statement, Brown now retracted it and said that he had not attacked either Ashton or Leatherbarrow, but instead it had been the Irish labourers who had come into his farmhouse and savagely beaten both men; and had threatened him, saying that he would get the same if he did not keep quiet. The police did not believe this story either and, on Thursday 29 September, John Brown was brought before the Ormskirk Magistrates' Court, formally charged with the murder of George Ashton.

An inquest was convened at the *Fox & Goose Inn*, Skelmersdale on the Thursday. The District Coroner, Mr Driffield, took charge of proceedings and John Brown was represented by a local solicitor by the name of France. When John Leatherbarrow gave evidence he still bore the scar on his forehead where Brown had struck him with the poker. He confirmed to the court that he had been employed by John Brown to operate the threshing machine along with Thomas Jardine, assisted by the deceased, George Ashton. Leatherbarrow described how he and Ashton had gone to the *Bowling Green Inn* at Dig Moor to give Brown his keys, and then gave a brief account of the initial confrontation between Brown and Ashton. Leatherbarrow was asked by the coroner had the confrontation been settled between the men, and Leatherbarrow said that it had been and that they had all walked back to Moss Brook Farm in good spirits. He then described how things had turned nasty once they were locked inside Brown's kitchen, explaining that Brown had begun drinking whisky and had suddenly lashed out with the poker, striking him over the head. Leatherbarrow told the court how he had grappled with Brown, wrenching the poker from his hands and had then forced Brown to unlock the door so as to escape. He confessed that in the heat of the moment he had forgotten all about Ashton and, once outside, had spent the night in the granary with Jardine.

Leatherbarrow's testimony continued. He informed the inquest that she had been up early and had reported the previous night's events to John Brown's son, Richard, before starting work on the threshing machine. Soon after, John Brown had appeared and had asked him if he was one of the men in his house last night. When Leatherbarrow confirmed that he was, Brown had punched him so hard in the face that it had knocked him off his feet. He said that Brown was about to 'lay into him', but some of the Irish labourers intervened and stopped him. Leatherbarrow then told the court that he had left the farm immediately after this confrontation, and had not been informed of George Ashton's death until late that evening.

The next witness was John Brown's eldest son, Richard, who explained to the court that there had been no disagreement between his father and Ashton, as he had been the one to fire

Ashton for drunkenness, not his father. He went on to recount the events of the day of the murder, and how he had given the keys to Ashton to hand to his father. When pressed, Richard Brown did say that when he had returned home later that night his father was in bed and he saw blood on the floor of the larder, but thought nothing of it.

When Thomas Jardine gave his evidence he told how Leatherbarrow had come into the granary on Monday night in a terrible state and had told him that he had been attacked by the farmer. He added that when he got up the following morning he too had been challenged by John Brown who, he said, was in a foul mood. He said that Brown had said to him: 'Where's that **** Leatherbarrow' and, fearing some violent retribution, he had pointed him in the right direction.

The Irish labourers also gave evidence, and they all gave similar accounts of the events. When they went inside the farm-house they discovered that the man was George Ashton, who was 'covered in blood'. They carried him into the barn and laid him down on the straw.

The police also gave their evidence. PC Chitson had been the first officer at the scene and had been led to the barn where he found Ashton lying on his back, his face covered with blood which had by this time dried and congealed. Walking into the farmhouse, he said that the kitchen was covered in blood, with splatters on the walls and floor.

The wounds inflicted to Ashton were explained to the court by the police surgeon, Dr Hilton, who had carried out a post-mortem examination of the body the day after the murder. He stated that Ashton had sustained several blows to the head and torso, fracturing the breastbone in the process. Dr Hilton confirmed that all of the injuries inflicted on the deceased were consistent to the use of heavy, blunt instruments. When pressed by the coroner, Dr Hilton elaborated, saying that the fatal blows to the head had most probably been from a metal bar, such as a poker, while the blows to the body had been from a much larger, flatter object. When asked could the deceased have been kicked or stamped on, the doctor confirmed that that was the most likely explanation. He added that the prisoner was a tall and heavily-built man, while the deceased was slight and would have had 'no possible chance in a struggle'. In answer to the coroner's final question: 'Could the victim have recovered from such a severe beating?' the doctor shook his head and replied 'No.'

The final police officer to take the witness stand was Sergeant Parker, who, along with PC Chitson, had arrested John Brown. He told the court that the accused was still in an intoxicated state when he had been apprehended. He also described the murder weapon, stating that they had found a bloodstained poker in the farmhouse with the end broken off. When the officer was asked: 'Could this damage have occurred as the result of striking a hard object with force?' he replied: 'Yes.'

Having now heard all of the evidence, the coroner concluded that there was nothing, in his opinion, to suggest that the death of George Ashton was the result of manslaughter. The jury concurred, finding John Brown guilty of the wilful murder of George Ashton. He was therefore committed on a coroner's warrant to stand trial at the forthcoming Liverpool Assizes.

John Brown appeared at Liverpool Assizes on 21 December 1869, and pleaded not guilty to the wilful murder of George Ashton. The evidence against Brown was overwhelming and

John Brown appeared at Liverpool Assizes on 21 December, 1869, and pleaded not guilty to the wilful murder of George Ashton.

made the prosecution's case, led by Mr Addison QC, easy. The defence counsel, led by Mr Pope QC, attempted to mitigate the situation by promoting the prisoner's previous good character and that the crime had been the result of intoxication. This tactic seemed to win over the judge, who reduced the charge to manslaughter. The jury concurred with the judge's direction and John Brown was sentenced to ten years' penal servitude.

CHAPTER 8

Possessed by the Demon Drink

1869

Ellen was screaming, and called for help from her neighbours.

Domestic violence has been a common theme running through many of the murders committed in Wigan. Violent husbands, many of them colliers, were driven, often when intoxicated, to savagely beat and kick their wives to death. The case of John and Ellen Gregson was no exception.

The couple, who had been married six years, lived in a humble dwelling at No 1 Wood's Yard, off Great George Street, close to the Wigan & Liverpool Railway. John Gregson, who worked as a collier for the Douglas Bank Colliery, was well known locally as being a drunkard and a lout; and a man with a very violent temper, especially after he had had a drink or two. He had attacked and beaten his wife on several previous occasions. Five years earlier Gregson was sentenced to six months in prison for assaulting her. He was well known to both the local constabulary and the magistrates, who considered him to be a habitual criminal; in fact, on the day in question, Monday 18 October 1869, he appeared before Wigan Magistrates' Court on a charge of being drunk and disorderly, let off with a fine.

Gregson had worked his shift at the Douglas Bank Colliery and, rather than returning home to his wife and their baby, went to the pub. When he did return home later that evening it was only because he had spent all of his money. He was in a drunken and abusive state as he entered the house. One of their neighbours, a Mrs Littler, had come around to see Ellen and their sixteen-month-old baby. Gregson accosted his wife, demanding that she take his coat down to the local pawn-brokers so he could have more money to continue his drinking spree. When she refused, he demanded that she leave home immediately.

Ellen, who was nursing their baby, scolded her husband for

Although in 1869 Great George Street was filled with terraced housing –
John and Ellen Gregson lived in a humble dwelling at No 1 Wood's Yard, off
Great George Street – today all those slums have long since been demolished
and Great George Street is filled with industrial units.

the manner in which he had spoken and behaved towards their
neighbour, but told him that she would take the coat down to
the pawnbrokers once she had finished feeding the child.
Impatient as ever, Gregson snatched the child from her arms,
telling her that he would take care of it while she went to the
pawnshop – now! Ellen then told him that she would pawn the

John Gregson – a collier for the Douglas Bank Colliery – was well known locally as being a drunkard and a lout, and a man that had a very violent temper, especially after he had had a drink or two.

coat, but the money would pay for food for the children and would not be wasted on ale. She took back the child and was about to place it in its cradle when he began to lay into her, knocking her to the floor and kicking her repeatedly.

Ellen screamed and called for help. A neighbour and fellow collier, Robert Hilton, heard the commotion and rushed in, pulling Gregson away. He fought him off and once more punched and kicked his wife. Hilton, who was now receiving a beating from Gregson, shouted to another neighbour, Maria Hurst, who was in the doorway, to help him and the two of them wrestled Gregson off his wife. Although Hilton had succeeded in calming the situation, Gregson refused to allow anyone to summon a doctor to attend to Ellen's wounds, saying that his wife would be fine. Gregson told Hilton to leave, and that was that.

Later that evening, Maria Hurst returned to the house to check on Ellen's condition. She discovered the young woman in bed, suffering terrible abdominal pain. She insisted on staying with her and sat beside her all through the night until the early hours of the following morning when she had to begin work at the local cotton mill.

At around 8.30 am, Ellen's sister, Alice, came by and finding her sister in severe pain insisted on summoning a doctor. Although the doctor came out to the house he decided that there was little he could do, besides prescribing a 'sixpenny worth of brandy'. Gregson returned home that evening and gave his wife the brandy. As he raised the cup to her lips she must have suffered a convulsion, as she bit the edge of the cup and a piece went into her mouth. Unable to take the piece out of her own mouth, she pleaded with John to do it for her. We can only guess that she was suffering a series of uncontrollable convulsions, as she bit his fingers as he attempted to take the shard from her mouth. Losing his temper, he grabbed a spoon and in a harsh and uncaring fashion began probing his wife's mouth in a vague attempt to free the loose piece. When Ellen then refused to open her mouth, John Gregson began striking her in the face and over the head with the spoon. Maria Hurst came in the room and begged him to stop before he killed her. Carefully tilting Ellen's head, Maria managed to extract the fragment of pottery with ease. Soon after, Alice returned, and Gregson began to curse her for summoning the doctor and wasting good brandy.

The following morning, once John Gregson had left for work at the pit, the neighbours came around to check on Ellen. Finding her in a very distressed state, they summoned the local surgeon. When Dr Jackson arrived later that day he was horrified to see the state that Ellen Gregson was in and, as he attempted to attend to her wounds and made arrangements for her to be taken to Wigan Dispensary, he had the neighbours summon the police. John Gregson was arrested at the colliery by PC Bisell and taken to the local police station were he was charged with assaulting his wife and causing actual bodily harm.

However, despite the best efforts of the nursing staff at the Dispensary, Ellen Gregson died there at 11 pm on Thursday 21 October, as a direct result of the injuries inflicted by her husband. Gregson was still in custody and the charge was subsequently raised to one of wilful murder.

Ralph Darlington, the Borough Coroner, convened an inquest into the death of Ellen Gregson on 25 October. Several of the Gregsons' neighbours gave evidence, including Maria Hurst and Robert Hilton, who offered background information

Wigan's modern Magistrates' Court on Darlington Street – John Gregson was a regular visitor to the town's Victorian predecessor and had appeared there on Monday 18 October 1869, just prior to the savage attack upon his wife.

regarding John Gregson's frequent violent outbursts, and described in detail the events of the evening of Monday 18 October. Mr Darlington challenged John Gregson over his actions and asked why he had stopped his neighbours from summoning a doctor to attend to his wife. Gregson replied that he didn't think she was that serious, and added: 'I thought she'd get better.' The local surgeon who had examined Ellen Gregson's body, found it had extensive bruising. Much more serious had been a blow to the head, delivered with such severity that it had fractured the base of her skull. The resulting haemorrhage had caused Ellen Gregson's eventual death. The jury were convinced that although Ellen Gregson had died sometime after the beating inflicted by her husband, he was responsible for her death, and they returned a verdict of guilty of wilful murder.

John Gregson appeared before Justice Baron Martin at the Liverpool Assizes on 17 December 1869, and entered a plea of not guilty. For the prosecution, led by Mr Leresche, it was an open and shut case; the prisoner had inflicted such savage and unprovoked beating upon his wife that she had died as a direct

Despite the best efforts of the nursing staff at the Dispensary, Ellen Gregson would die there at 11 pm on Thursday 21 October as a direct result of the injuries inflicted by her husband.

result of her injuries. The prisoner was therefore guilty of the murder of his wife, Ellen Gregson.

The defence, led by Mr Torr, attempted to muddy the waters, suggesting that if the accused had only beaten his wife to chastise her and had had no intention of killing her then that was not murder. This line of defence seemed to confuse the jury who felt the need to ask the judge, Mr Justice Baron Martin, to clarify what was and was not murder in the eyes of the law.

However, the judge's responses to the jury's question seemed to be in a manner that revealed that he had little sympathy for the accused and, for the most part, he was advising the jury that regardless of Gregson's actual intent, to beat his wife so severely that it led to her death was murder. The judge's comments even provoked Mr Torr, counsel for the defence, to question what was and was not murder in the eyes of the law, though the judge seemingly dismissed his response. It was little wonder then that the jury returned a guilty verdict; though Mr Torr's pleas for leniency must have gravitated with the collective conscience of the jury, as they recommended that the judge be merciful in his sentencing. Justice Baron Martin chose to ignore the jury's

John Gregson appeared before Justice Baron Martin at the Liverpool Assizes on 17 December 1869.

caveat and, donning his black cap, sentenced John Gregson to death.

There was great disquiet at the verdict, and the local press had a field day, challenging the sentence and championing Gregson's case for leniency. The Wigan papers were quick to compare this case to that of Up Holland farmer, John Brown, who had beaten George Ashton to death with a poker while intoxicated. In that case, Mr Justice Baron Martin had ruled that Brown could not be found guilty of wilful murder as he was under the influence of alcohol at the time he committed the crime. Now, the same judge was sentencing a man to death for beating his wife to death while intoxicated. The Press inferred that both decisions had been judged on the basis of status and class – Brown was a farmer, a landowner and a man of wealth and status, while Gregson was merely a working-class man, an illiterate collier – and not the law and justice. And yet, although the Press were now taking the moral high ground on Gregson's behalf, at the time of the murder they had been much more scathing of the conduct of the working classes. For example, referring to the brutality and mindlessness of the case, the

Gazette had commented that: 'Surely the frequent occurrence of such cases of these shows a state of mind amongst the lower orders that is sufficiently ominous.'

Nevertheless, in spite of the best actions of the friends and family of John Gregson – who had raised a petition containing literally hundreds of names, which they sent to the Home Secretary in the hope of having his sentence reduced – the sentence stood, and at 8 am on 10 January 1870, twenty-eight-year-old John Gregson was executed at Kirkdale Prison for the callous and wilful murder of his wife, Ellen, on 21 October 1869.

CHAPTER 9

The Odd Confession

1871

She lived with her stepfather openly as 'man and wife'

Under normal circumstances, the police are aware that a murder has been committed when a crime or the discovery of a body is reported to them. Occasionally, however, the crime has been committed without anyone else being aware of it, and if the body remains undiscovered then the murderer can avoid detection. Equally, a person can be murdered, but because the death appears to be unsuspicious and of natural causes the murder can go undetected. It's much rarer for the murderer to walk into a police station and offer up a confession to the police. That was exactly what happened on 1 July 1871.

Early on a Saturday morning, a mature woman walked into King Street police station and asked to speak to the Chief Constable, William Simm. The desk sergeant attempted to dissuade her from this and said that the Chief Constable was a very busy man, and that rather than bother him unnecessarily, he would be happy to deal with the matter himself. The woman was undeterred, insisting that she had something very important to report, but she would only do this to the Chief Constable himself. With great reluctance, the desk sergeant informed Mr Simm of the situation, and the Chief Constable decided that he would see the woman.

She told Chief Constable Simm that her name was Anne Burns, was sixty-two years of age, from 10 John Street, Wigan where she had lived for more than thirty years, with her mother and stepfather, Edward McGravey. She told him that her relationship with McGravey was not that of father to daughter. Instead, almost from the day he had married her mother, she had become his lover. Furthermore, this relationship had not only been conducted with the full knowledge of her mother, but seemingly with her full approval. The relationship had actually produced a number of children and, since her mother's death in

The little old lady who walked into King Street police station on the morning of Saturday 1 July 1871 would have a very 'odd confession' to make to the Chief Constable, William Simm.

1846, she had lived with McGravey as 'husband and wife' and had been accepted by the neighbours and the community as a whole. The couple continued to live together until Edward McGravey's death in 1870.

It was about Edward McGravey's death that she had come to see the Chief Constable. Anne Burns informed William Simm that she had 'come for the purpose of surrendering herself for having murdered her stepfather'. She went on to say that the murder had been playing on her conscience for some time, to the point that it was beginning to affect her health. Anne Burns went on to explain that Mr McGravey had been ill, and had been attended by the late Dr Reilly, the union medical officer acting for the borough. Anne had been nursing him at home alone but had become tired of the very stressful situation. Knowing that his life was insured, she had decided to murder him. As she was preparing his food it had been quite easy for her to give him poisons that would hasten his death.

She told the Chief Constable that she had begun to poison Mr McGravey about a fortnight before his eventual demise. It

All the houses that once stood on John Street – including No 10, the former home of sixty-two-year-old Anne Burns – have long since been demolished and only a short section of the street survives today as an entrance to an infants school.

had begun one evening when the deceased had been sitting in his armchair by the fireside and had asked for his medicine. Anne added washing liquor to the mixture and gave it to him in a cup. Finding the washing liquor to be 'not sufficiently potent', about a week later she purchased 'a pennyworth of white precipitate' which she had administered to Mr McGravey in warm water. The process was repeated about a week later. After giving the second dose, she had become concerned that it might be discovered so she threw the remaining white powder away. The precipitate seemed to have been the final straw, as within the week seventy-year-old Edward McGravey became seriously ill and died on 5 July 1870. His physician, Dr Reilly, was summoned and, putting the death down to disease of the bladder, confirmed this on the death certificate.

Anne Burns told Chief Constable Simm that she had claimed on her stepfather's life insurance and three separate companies had paid out the money without any questions being asked: £19 from the Prudential Insurance Club, £6 from the United Assurance Club and a further £4 5s from a local 'family in-surance club'. Although she had got away with her stepfather's

murder and had benefited from the crime, the facts of what she
had actually done began to play on her mind. Over the period
since his death Anne Burns had had trouble sleeping, and as
things began to get on top of her, she had come to the decision
that she must confess.

The Chief Constable, who had listened patiently to her
confession and had carefully written it all down, now read it
back to her. When he finished he asked her if it was correct and
she replied: 'It's perfectly right.' He now informed her that
confessing to a murder was something that the police took very
seriously indeed and while the facts of what she had claimed
would be investigated thoroughly she would have to remain in
custody. Anne Burns signed the statement and was taken to a
cell. Preliminary enquiries confirmed that it had been open
knowledge that Anne Burns had been living with Edward
McGravey as man and wife, and they had brought up five children together. Their neighbours spoke highly of her, saying that
she was a decent woman and was very well liked locally.

On the morning of Monday 3 July 1871, Anne Burns
appeared before local magistrates J Lamb, R Burland and W
Melling, and was formally charged with the murder of Edward
McGravey. The Chief Constable, William Simm, carefully read
out the notes of the confession which she had given to him on
the Saturday morning and, as his officers needed more time to
investigate the case, he asked that she remain in custody. The
magistrates agreed to this request. However, Mr Simm was not
finished, and informed the Bench that he had a more shocking
revelation to tell the court. He went on to explain that while
Anne Burns had been led into court she had asked to speak to
him again and, to his great surprise, stated:

> *I did not tell you all I did. I murdered my two children I had by
> McGravey about thirty years ago. My mother knew about them.
> She buried the first, but I do not know where, and some other
> women buried the other. We lived at Dan McAnnally's when I
> had the first, and at No 10 John Street when I had the second.*

When Anne Burns walked into King Street police station she
had been in a deeply troubled and depressed state. Throughout
the proceedings she kept her face muffled in a shawl, which was
only removed once when one of the wardens removed it for a
brief moment – but she quickly covered herself up again. It was
remarked that 'she seemed very haggard and care worn, and

wore during the hearing a listless look'. During her time in custody and particularly since she made the second confession, her mental state had deteriorated further. Mr Simm became deeply concerned about the state of her health, particularly as she was now refusing to eat. Simm instructed the police surgeon to examine her. Although she behaved in a rational manner, the surgeon was of the opinion that she was suffering from depression. The cells of King Street police station were no worse than any other Victorian police station, but under the circumstances they were considered far from suitable for her continued detention. After consulting with Nathaniel Eckersley, the Mayor of Wigan, the Chief Constable took the unusual step of having the prisoner transferred to the Union Workhouse on Frog Lane. Here, although she would still be detained, she would be free to converse with the other inmates. However, despite the change in her surroundings, Anne Burns's mental state continued to deteriorate at a pace. Within a matter of weeks she had become completely incoherent.

After consulting with Nathaniel Eckersley, Mayor of Wigan, the Chief Constable took the unusual step of having the prisoner transferred to the Union Workhouse on Frog Lane. The Workhouse closed in 1930, initially becoming the Frog Lane Public Assistance Institution, before it became Frog Lane Welfare Home under the NHS. It finally closed its doors in 1970 and, following demolition, housing was built in its place.

Anne Burns was committed to the Lancashire County Lunatic Asylum on 19 July 1871. The institution, which came under the control of the NHS and was renamed Rainhill Hospital, closed in 1991 under the 'Care in the Community' programme. The buildings were later demolished and a housing estate now occupies the site. The only surviving aspect is the former perimeter wall.

The police investigations were not going very well. Although Mr Simm had wanted McGravey's body exhumed from its grave in the Borough cemetery, he had been informed that it would be far from straightforward. Other burials had been laid over that of Mr McGravey so to exhume him they would have to exhume others. Equally, there was a distinct lack of witnesses to either of the murdered children and little hope of ever discovering where they had been buried. When Mr Simm reported his findings to the local magistrates they were all of a mind that it would be better for all concerned if the case was closed.

In the meantime, Anne Burns' health continued to decline. Dr Smallman, acting for the Union Workhouse, informed Mr Simm that, in his opinion, she was now on the verge of insanity and it would be best if she was committed to the Lancashire County Lunatic Asylum at Rainhill. This substantial building, opened on 1 January 1851, initially housed 750 patients. Designed by Liverpool architect, G E Grayson, Rainhill became the main psychiatric institution for the whole of

Lancashire. Such was its catchment area that rising demand meant that the building had to be extended in 1860 and 1886. Matters were put in place, and on 19 July 1871, Anne Burns was transferred to Rainhill. She never recovered from the guilt of her actions and died there within two years.

CHAPTER 10

Without Provocation

1887

The police discovered Mrs Atherton lying dead on the kitchen floor, her body battered and heavily bloodstained

Wigan found economic success as an industrial town during the eighteenth century, and people from across Lancashire and even further afield came in search of employment. An acute housing shortage, lasting well into the nineteenth century, meant that many new inhabitants were forced to rent space within an existing household. Indeed, the desire to 'take in lodgers' was something that continued in towns like Wigan throughout the nineteenth and well into the twentieth century.

Henry Atherton and his wife, Margaret, had lived in St Helens for several years before moving to Ince to seek employment. The couple lodged at a terraced house in Back Broom Street, owned by Jane Brown. Henry was unskilled and found work where he could, as a common labourer. Throughout his forty-five year life Henry gained a reputation as being a bit of a bully, prone to easily losing his temper over the slightest matter and it was said by many that knew him that he gave his wife, Margaret, a 'dog's life'. The couple's stay with Mrs Brown was short and, by all accounts was to be terminated within a couple of days, on the suspicion that they were responsible for a shawl going missing.

On Saturday 21 November, Henry returned from work as usual and had his evening meal in the kitchen with his wife and Mrs Brown. Later there was a knock at the door and Henry answered it, soon returning to the kitchen with a man he introduced as a friend, named Sturgeon. All four sat in the kitchen throughout the remainder of the evening, drinking beer and talking. Mrs Brown would later recall that the mood seemed uplifted and bright. Later on she retired to bed for the night and left Mr and Mrs Atherton along with their guest still drinking in the kitchen.

Whether the mood changed after Mrs Brown had gone to bed is uncertain, but what is known is that by the time Henry had gone upstairs to the couple's bedroom to collect some matches and come down again his mood had most certainly changed. He was now very angry indeed. What had triggered this sudden change of mood remains uncertain – perhaps he had discovered the missing shawl that his wife had adamantly denied stealing, the suspicion of which was the reason they would soon be looking for new lodgings – but he suddenly began cursing and swearing at his wife and, without any warning, started hitting and kicking her with great violence. Sturgeon stood by and did nothing, he did not attempt to calm the situation, nor did he try to intervene and stop Henry Atherton from raining down a barrage of kicks and blows on his wife who, by now, was on the floor.

Whether Margaret Atherton was alive or dead when Sturgeon left the house that night remains uncertain. Atherton would later claim that she was, though having suffered what can only be described as a severe beating, it is hard to see that she could possibly be alive. When Sturgeon did leave he reported the incident to the police, who came around to the house at once. When the police officers arrived they found the house in darkness, and had to bang hard on the front door for several minutes before it was opened by Mr Atherton. The police discovered Mrs Atherton lying dead on the kitchen floor, her body battered and heavily bloodstained. Atherton followed the police into the kitchen and seemed remarkably calm. The police arrested Henry Atherton for the wilful murder of his wife, Margaret, and took him to the local police station.

When questioned, Henry Atherton denied any involvement in the murder of his wife, and also that he had beaten her. He claimed that he had gone to bed early that evening, leaving his wife in the kitchen with Sturgeon and Mrs Brown, and had only discovered that she was dead when the police had woken him from a deep sleep by banging on the door. This version of events was later refuted by both Mrs Brown and Sturgeon.

Charged with the wilful murder of his wife, without the slightest provocation, on Saturday 21 November 1887, Henry Atherton appeared at Liverpool Assizes, held at St George's Hall. Mr Watson, the leading prosecution barrister, opened the case by calling the prisoner's brother Edward. He testified that his brother was a troubled man, and that their father had been declared as being insane some years earlier. However, Edward

Charged with the wilful murder of his wife, without the slightest provocation, on Saturday 21 November 1887, Henry Atherton appeared at Liverpool Assizes, held at St George's Hall.

Atherton went on to say that although his brother was no angel, he had never witnessed any ill-treatment or assault on his wife.

When Sturgeon appeared in the witness box he came under a great deal of criticism for his actions on the evening in question, or rather his apparent inaction in even attempting to step in and prevent Atherton from kicking his wife to death. Sturgeon defended himself by stating that he did not consider it his place to interfere in the domestic situation between a husband and wife. Jane Brown, the Athertons' landlady was also called to give evidence in the witness box, and confirmed that she had given the Athertons notice to quit on the suspicion of stealing the missing shawl. She went on to describe the couple's relationship, describing Henry Atherton's personality as volatile, whereas Margaret Atherton was very quiet and subservient to her husband. On the night in question she told the court that she had retired to bed but sometime later had been awoken by what she described as a heated argument downstairs, and recalled hearing Henry Atherton shouting what had sounded like 'Mag is dead'. The police surgeon, Dr Lang, who had examined the deceased's body, informed the court that

Margaret Atherton had suffered a severe beating, explaining that there were large bruises all over her body, in his opinion inflicted as a result of savage kicking by heavy work boots or clogs. He went on to say that the fatal blow had been a kick to the side of the head which had resulted in a haemorrhage.

The defence counsel, led by Mr Segar, had an uphill struggle to convince the jury of the prisoner's innocence. They chose not to call any witnesses, not even their client, who was seen visibly shaking in the dock. Instead, Segar addressed his comments directly to the jury. Accepting that his client was without doubt responsible for the murder, he pleaded the case that at the time of the fatal attack the prisoner was not aware of his actions. He did not go so far as to suggest insanity, but that was the general impression he was trying to convey.

In his summing up, the judge pointed out to the jury that, if the accused had acted intentionally on the night in question, then he was surely guilty of the murder of Margaret Atherton. However, if, as the defence had suggested, the accused was not in his own mind and incapable of knowing his own actions when he attacked his wife, then they should return a verdict of manslaughter. The jury retired to consider their verdict. Within thirty minutes they returned. The foreman said that the accused was guilty of manslaughter. When asked did he have anything to say before the sentence was passed, Henry Atherton simply shook his head. The judge told him that he had, in a moment of apparent madness, delivered a depraved and unprovoked attack on his wife causing her death and that he would go to prison for twenty years.

CHAPTER 11

The Rape and Murder of a Child

1890

The eight-year-old girl had not only been battered to death but raped

Hannah Lydia Birchall was illegitimate. Following the death of her father, she had been raised by her mother, Anne, who subsequently married local collier William Dickinson. They moved into Dickinson's home on Petticoat Lane, Ince. Since their marriage in the summer of 1888, the couple had had two children together, one almost a year old, the other still a babe in arms. The family had been together for almost two years by the time Hannah disappeared, on Wednesday 5 March 1890.

The Dickinsons were a poor family. Although William worked at Moss Hall Colliery, his wage was not great and continued absences reduced the family income even further. On the day in question the family were once again suffering financial hardship and, following an argument with her husband, Mrs Dickinson agreed to take a jacket to the local pawnbrokers in order to generate some cash. Departing the family home around 6.30 pm, she left the two youngest children upstairs, while Hannah was downstairs with her stepfather.

Mrs Dickinson was gone a while as she had had to haggle the best price she could get from the pawnbroker. When she returned Mr Dickinson was still in the house, but little Hannah was nowhere to be seen. When she asked her husband where Hannah was he replied that she had 'gone outside to play'. At first Anne Dickinson did not question her daughter's disappearance, even though it had been dark outside for several hours and a cold night. Later, however, as the night progressed and Hannah did not return, she became more anxious, and decided to walk to the local police station to report her daughter's disappearance.

Although the police took the matter seriously – Mrs

The appearance of Petticoat Lane, the former home of William and Anne Dickinson, has changed considerably through the years since the horrific death of Hannah Lydia Birchall and the only former colliers' cottages that survive today are those located at Islands Brow.

The former County Police Station at Ince, where Mrs Dickinson reported the disappearance of her daughter.

Dickinson did not suspect anything suspicious – they regarded the matter as a missing child and did not begin any search until the following morning. Then, police numbers were swelled by a great many local volunteers who had come along to search for the missing girl. The teams spread out and covered the immediate area before extending their search. They looked in all the obvious places where a small child could be hiding, checking yards and outbuildings, even dragging the local section of the Leeds & Liverpool Canal – but there was still no sign of Hannah.

Amongst the many volunteers was Peter Dickinson, William's brother, who was one of the men searching the property to the rear of Petticoat Lane. On derelict land to the back of the houses were the remains of the old Ravine Pit. Its long-disused shaft had been covered in boulders and a brick wall erected around it, topped with an iron grating. While searching the derelict buildings close by, Peter noticed that some of the boulders had been moved, and a closer inspection found hairs caught on the bars of the grating. Rather than reporting this important discovery direct to one of the police officers searching in the immediate vicinity, Peter instead chose to keep the information to himself and only later that evening did he pass on his findings to his brother, William. The two men discussed whether the missing girl could have fallen down the shaft and if they should inform the police. In the end it was William, the missing girl's stepfather, who decided that the police should be told and he assured Peter that he would be the one to do it. However, William waited until late the following evening before walking around to Ince police station. The police inspected the shaft on the Saturday morning and, although they realised the significance of the discovery, they were also very much aware that exploring the shaft would take time: the rubble covering the mouth would need to be cleared and, as the disused mine shaft was almost three hundred feet deep, specialist equipment was required to make a descent; and an experienced person needed for the potentially dangerous task. The police had to wait until the following morning before a rig could be set up, and then a local ex-miner, James Orrell, volunteered to be lowered down the shaft. The descent was slow and perilous; however, when Orrell reached the bottom a grisly discovery was made. Through the gloom he noticed a hand protruding from accumulated debris. Closer inspection revealed that it was the body of the missing girl, Hannah Birchall. Orrell gave the signal to ascend and returned to the surface to give the police and the large crowd of onlookers the terrible news. Later, he would descend the shaft for a second time, in order to recover Hannah's body.

Closer examination of the girl's body revealed that she had not only been battered to death, but had been raped. Although the clothes she was last seen wearing were missing, her under-clothes had no trace of blood on them. It was clear to the police that whoever had raped and murdered the young girl had also redressed her before tossing the body down the old shaft. The obvious suspect was her stepfather, William Dickinson, as it was common knowledge that he resented having to raise another man's child. Police arrested Dickinson immediately and took him to Ince police station for questioning.

The disappearance of little Hannah was met with shock and horror by the local community of Ince, and this had been clearly reflected in the large number of local people who had come out on to the streets and volunteered to help search for the missing girl. Now that her body had been discovered, just a few hundred yards from her home on Petticoat Lane, and hearing the dreadful news that she had been raped and murdered, the community was deeply shocked and very emotional. This emotion would turn to anger once news of Dickinson's arrest was circulated. A large and angry crowd gathered outside Ince police station on the Sunday evening. The local police were so concerned that a riot might occur that they called for reinforcements from neighbouring stations, and Dickinson was formally charged with the rape and wilful murder of his stepdaughter in the police court rather than risk transferring him to the magistrates' court in Wigan.

A coroner's inquest was convened at the *Prince of Wales Hotel*, Ince on Tuesday 18 March. Some interesting evidence emerged. The police surgeon, for example, confirmed that the girl had been raped, and had then been killed by a blow to the head. However, as the contusion to the skull had been obliterated as a result of the intense damage inflicted to the girl's skull as a result of being pushed down the mine shaft, they were not able to suggest what had been the murder weapon.

Several of the Dickinsons' neighbours testified to the court of the 'awkward' relationship that existed between Hannah and her stepfather. However, it was the testimony of another neighbour, Eunice Taylor, who first suggested that Mrs Dickinson might also have been involved in her daughter's murder. She informed the court that Mrs Dickinson had asked her to clean the parlour on the very day that they were about to begin descending the shaft to look for Hannah's body. This suggested that Mrs Dickinson was already aware that her daughter had been pushed down the shaft. When Mr Brighthouse, the county coroner, put this question to the witness, Eunice Taylor agreed. She also confirmed that the family often quarrelled over Hannah, and that William Dickinson seemed to have little time for the child. Another neighbour, Anne Whiteside, told the court that she had visited the Dickinson home on the day of the big search and had seen Mrs Dickinson washing clothes in the dolly tub which contained 'blood-red water'. However, despite testimony that seemed to implicate Anne Dickinson in the disappearance and subsequent murder of her daughter, the coroner was far from convinced and even directed the jury that, in his opinion, there was no case against the child's mother. The jury did, however, return a verdict of wilful murder against William Dickinson. And yet the greatest surprise came the following day when Mrs Dickinson, who had been exonerated by the coroner, was arrested by police and charged with her

The Dickinsons' trial began at the Liverpool Assizes on 16 May 1890.

daughter's murder. Both Mr and Mrs Dickinson would stand trial at the next Liverpool Assizes.

The Dickinsons' trial began on 16 May. Almost immediately, Mr Dickinson's defence counsel pointed out to the judge that at the coroner's inquest Mrs Dickinson had given evidence that was prejudicial to her husband's defence, and as they were now being tried for the same crime it was only right and proper that they should be tried separately. The judge, Mr Justice Baron Huddlestone, agreed and Mrs Dickinson was led out of the dock to be tried at a later date.

The prosecution set out a case that the only person who could have raped and murdered Hannah was her stepfather. The child could not have removed the boulders from around the mine shaft herself as they were far too heavy. If someone else had committed the crime then why should they bother to dress the child in new, clean undergarments? The evidence pointed to the stepfather, William Dickinson, being the guilty party. He would have had the opportunity to commit the crime during the absence of his wife; he had access to the change of undergarments, and could then have disposed of her body down the shaft. And there was the bloodstained water in the dolly tub that had been witnessed by Mrs Whiteside the day after the girl's disappearance. The prosecuting counsel also pointed to the obvious delay in reporting the fact that his brother had discovered the disturbed boulders around the mouth of the shaft and the hairs on the grating.

Meanwhile, the defence began to sow a seed of honest doubt in the mind of the jury, by saying that there was no compelling evidence to connect their client with the disappearance, rape or murder of Hannah. And, in spite of the way he may have felt towards the girl, it was unthinkable that a man like Dickinson would rape and murder his own stepdaughter. It was more likely to be the act of a stranger. They gave the jury a more credible alternative to consider: a mysterious tramp-like figure had been seen around Ince on the very day that Hannah had gone missing, and it made much more sense to imagine that it was the tramp, who had in fact abducted, raped and murdered the girl, not her stepfather as the prosecution suggested. Their tactics seemed to have convinced the jury, as they took everyone in the court by surprise when they returned a verdict of not guilty.

The case aroused great emotion within the local community. Many of the Dickinsons' neighbours travelled to Liverpool to watch the trial. When the verdict was given there was uproar, and when William Dickinson walked free from the court he was pursued to Lime Street Station by an angry and menacing crowd. Fearing for his life, Dickinson summoned the police, who escorted him to Edge Hill Station, just outside Liverpool, where he caught the train home to Wigan. Mrs Dickinson was exonerated of all implications of the murder of her daughter. No one was ever arrested for the rape and murder of young Hannah Birchall.

CHAPTER 12

Street Fighting

1893

A 'kicking game' known as 'purring'

Wigan was transformed by the Industrial Revolution. Thousands of people flooded into the town in search of work in cotton mills and coal mines. Industrial Lancashire, the workshop of the world, attracted people from far and wide, including many Europeans seeking employment. Many Wiganers despised the so-called 'foreigners' and showed great hostility towards them. Even so, the events in 1893 shocked the native inhabitants.

Wigan's Spring Fair, held in early May in the town's market

The market place had been the traditional venue for the town's Spring Fair held in early May.

Pasquale Panozzi and his fellow companions had been to the fair and began to make their way home along Standishgate, one of Wigan's traditional thoroughfares.

place, was a popular outing for the vast majority of the town's population. Pasquale Panozzi, an organ grinder, and his companions were there, walking along Standishgate and through the back streets on the edge of the district of Scholes at around 9 pm on Thursday 11 May. They were making their way back to their lodgings on Warrington Lane when a group of local children began to tease them. At first they took this in good humour, but soon the playful mood took a more sinister tone when the youngsters began shouting abuse. Initially, they ignored the taunts and walked on, but several of the children followed them and began throwing mud and stones. Panozzi and one of his companions responded to the volley of missiles by charging at the children in an attempt to catch them and, perhaps, give them a 'clip around the ear'. The Italians' actions were condemned by a group of locals standing outside the *Whitesmith's Arms* on Warrington Lane. One of the bystanders, Bernard Keenan, a collier, rushed up to the Italians and shouted at them to leave the kids alone.

Keenan then challenged Panozzi to a fight, a duel of wits

known as 'purring'. Purring was a common practice in rough and ready, working-class towns, such as St Helens, Warrington and Wigan. Street fighting was common, and one of the popular aspects of this urban violence was a 'kicking game'. Clogs were the favoured footwear of the day in Lancashire, and opponents would kick each other's shins as hard as they could until one of them could no longer stand up. The 'last man standing', as it were, was the victor. It was a stupid, mindless and very violent pursuit, which often had serious consequences.

Panozzi had a very poor grasp of the English language and was unable to understand what Keenan was asking him. By now several of the people standing outside the public house had crossed the road to join Keenan and, to the Italians, it must have appeared as though they had got themselves into trouble. As Keenan closed upon him, Panozzi, undoubtedly feeling intimidated and under immediate attack, lashed out wildly, striking him on the nose. Keenan responded by kicking the Italian hard in the shins. With this, Panozzi pulled a knife out of his jacket pocket and, as Keenan took a flying kick at him, he lashed out with the knife. It was more by fluke than intention that the blow connected, stabbing the collier in the chest with

Warrington Lane, the location where Pasquale Panozzi got into a tragic altercation with Bernard Keenan on Thursday 11 May 1893.

such force that the knife penetrated right up to the hilt, just below the heart. Keenan fell back into the arms of John Green, one of several men stood around watching the encounter, before collapsing to the floor, instantly bleeding from the deep wound. Panozzi, realising what he had just done, ran away, along with the other Italians. Meanwhile, the crowd gathered around Keenan.

Realising that he was in a serious condition, several of the group, including Green, Alexander Arbuthnot, James Andrews, Thomas Lofts and Thomas Taylor, all from the Warrington Lane area, picked Keenan up and carried him to Dr Monk's surgery. Despite the best efforts of Dr Monk's assistant, Keenan died within a few minutes.

The police were summoned and PCs Ryan and Barbour, who had been on patrol at Scholes Bridge, arrived on the scene within minutes, only to discover that the murderer had fled. While PC Barbour went around to Dr Monk's surgery, PC Ryan began searching for the assailant. He was soon directed to Mrs Bannond's lodging house on Warrington Lane, where an angry crowd was causing a disturbance. Following the stabbing, the Italians had departed the scene and returned to the lodging house. The large and very volatile crowd had followed the men and was now massing outside, baying for blood. To PC Ryan the situation had all the hallmarks of a lynch mob and, although he could not get them to disperse, he did manage to exert some control. Once inside, PC Ryan attempted to question the Italians, but because of their poor English this soon proved pointless. PC Ryan arrested Panozzi, who submitted without any fuss, and he escorted him to King Street police station. The lodging house crowd followed.

Once at the police station the prisoner was searched and amongst his possessions was a small buckhorn-handled knife which had fresh bloodstains on the blade. The police officers soon realised that Panozzi's lack of English was hampering their questioning, so Joseph Cassinelli was brought over from Standish to act as an interpreter. When the twenty-three-year-old Panozzi was charged with the wilful murder of thirty-year-old Bernard Keenan, he responded, through the interpreter, by asking: 'Do you mean to say that I thrust him with the knife?'

The murder aroused a great deal of interest in the town. When Panozzi appeared before Mr C Graham at the Wigan Magistrates' Court on Friday 12 May, a large crowd had gathered outside the building early, and rushed inside once the doors were opened. Joseph Cassinelli was sworn in to act as the prisoner's interpreter and he conveyed the case to Panozzi, sentence by sentence, throughout the hearing. Captain Bell, Wigan's chief constable, laid out the facts of the case to the magistrate and asked that the prisoner be kept on remand.

Several witnesses were called, including Mary Costello, the wife of Hugh Costello, a local collier, who had been outside the *Whitesmith's Arms* on the night of the murder. She informed the court that she had seen the two men get into a confrontation, and that the prisoner had struck the deceased on the nose just prior to the fatal stabbing. When the chief constable asked her had she seen the knife, she replied that she had and added that the prisoner had 'opened the knife and struck Keenan in the chest with it'. When Captain Bell asked: 'What sort of a knife was it?' the witness replied: 'A pocket knife.' The case was adjourned and Panozzi was remanded in custody pending an inquest.

The inquest was convened by Mr L R Rowbottom, the Borough Coroner, at Wigan Police Court on Saturday 20 May, where it was established that Bernard Keenan had died as a result of a single stab wound, penetrating the chest between the second and third rib. Several witnesses were called to give evidence, including John Green, Alexander Arbuthnot, and the victim's cousin, Margaret Leigh, who confirmed that Bernard Keenan, who had been staying at the *Britannia Inn* on Warrington Lane, could be violent when drunk. Although there was some dispute as to whether Keenan had responded in retaliation after Panozzi had struck him on the nose – some witnesses claimed that he had, while others said that he had not – all of the witnesses confirmed that they had seen the Italian plunge the knife into Keenan's chest before fleeing the scene. The jury returned a verdict of wilful murder and case was referred to Liverpool Assizes.

The case came before Justice Lawrence at the Liverpool Assizes on 31 July 1893. Pasquale Panozzi, who was described as an organ grinder, was charged with 'felonious murder with a knife' to which he pleaded not guilty. The case hinged on whether the prisoner had used the knife in self-defence or with malicious intent. The court heard that stone throwing was commonplace in Wigan, and that the act of 'purring' (which had to be explained to the judge, who was unfamiliar with either the term or the practice) was equally common. The prosecution, led by Mr Addison QC, claimed that Keenan had not rebuked the Italian for chasing the stone-throwing boys, but merely told him not to bother. In that instance, it had been the Italian who had attacked Keenan by striking him hard on the nose. And, not satisfied with that, had pulled out a knife and stabbed him to death. There was no provocation on Keenan's part, therefore, it was not a matter of self-defence, but wilful and cold blooded murder.

The defence counsel, led by Mr O'Feeley, painted a very different picture. He told the court that the accused and his companions had only lived in the town for a few days, unwittingly taking lodgings in Scholes, one of the worst areas of Wigan for violence. On the night in question they had been quietly walking home when they had come under attack, first from the stone-throwing boys, and then by an aggressive drunkard who liked to indulge in street fighting. O'Feeley also laboured the point that his client was a mild-mannered man who had not previously been in trouble with the law, while the victim (as the court had already heard from the police) was a man with a very violent character who was well known to the police and had been charged with assault on several previous occasions. Both of Panozzi's companions, Mr Pesci and Mr Morelli, gave evidence to the court and confirmed that when they had been challenged by the victim they had not understood his intentions, and thought that he was going to chastise them for chasing the boys who had hurled the stones. O'Feeley said that his client's actions could only be construed as self-defence, and that it was manslaughter and not murder.

Although the jury returned a verdict of manslaughter, a special plea was made that mercy and leniency should be shown to the prisoner. In passing sentence, Justice Lawrence told Panozzi (through an interpreter) that he had taken into account the jury's wishes, so he was to serve six months of hard labour.

CHAPTER 13

The Murder of a Detective

1895

I did it, I did it, not our Bill. So kill me, kill me!

For some time, the goods yards alongside the Wigan, London & North Western railway station were the scene of intense and regular theft. Most of the activities took place at weekends, during the early hours of the morning. Wagons were forced open and goods, worth a considerable amount of money, stolen. Despite the best efforts of Wigan's railway police, the thieves had neither been caught nor dissuaded from their criminal activities. With such a wave of thefts, the L & NWR Company instructed its officers to mount a concerted effort to apprehend the villains and put a stop to the thefts once and for all.

So serious was the level of criminality on railway property within the town that Wigan's railway police called on the services and support of the neighbouring Manchester force. With an incident having already occurred on the night of Saturday 28 September 1895, arrangements were made for Manchester's Detective Sergeant Kidd to come over the following evening to assist the local officer, DC William Osborne. DS Robert Kidd, who lived in Salford, worked for the railway police, for the London & North Western Railway Company (L&NWR). He was a hard-working and well-respected officer, and no stranger to Wigan, as he had been called upon for advice and to act as a liaison between the neighbouring forces on many previous occasions. Thirty-seven-year-old Kidd was a proud family man, the father of seven young children. Little did he know when he departed Manchester for Wigan on a fateful Sunday evening that this would prove to be his last ever visit to the town. Within minutes of his arrival he was brutally murdered by a ruthless gang of thieves.

DC Osborne met DS Robert Kidd off the 8 pm train and the two policemen discussed the case and their course of action,

Wigan's London & North Western railway station, where DC William Osborne met DS Robert Kidd who had travelled over from Salford to assist in the investigation of the continuing thefts from the neighbouring goods yard.

The former goods yard of the L&NWR where the attack on DS Kidd took place and Chapel Lane where the culprits entered the yard.

whilst proceeding to the nearby goods yard. Although Kidd had decided that the best strategy was to mount a stake-out, when the pair arrived at the goods yard they could clearly hear the sound of wood breaking, coming from the far side of the yard. Keeping low, they made their way along the exterior wall. As they reached the end of the wall they could clearly see one man standing as a look-out. DC Osborne immediately challenged him, asking what he was doing there. However, as Osborne attempted to arrest the suspicious man two more men appeared. These, who had been attempting to break into a railway wagon, began attacking the police officer. Although Osborne drew his truncheon, it was knocked out of his hand by one of the assailants.

Meanwhile, Kidd chased after a group of other men who were now trying to make good their escape. Although some of them ran away into the night, others stood their ground and fought with the detectives. The two officers were clearly out-numbered and the encounter soon went the way of the thieves. During an intense and violent scuffle Robert Kidd was stabbed several times and fell to the ground. Meanwhile, DC Osborne was also taking quite a severe beating. With both of the officers unable to continue the pursuit, the thieves ran away.

Detective Constable Osborne had been severely injured during the attack and lost consciousness. When he finally came to he saw his colleague, DS Kidd, on his hands and knees, in a pool of blood. As Osborne approached him, he was still conscious and said: 'Is that you, Osborne?' The latter replied: 'Yes.' Kidd then asked his colleague for a drink of water, but lost consciousness soon afterwards. Although he did what he could to save him, Osborne was unable to stem the flow of blood from the fatal neck wound. He attempted to lift and carry his colleague to safety, but found the strain just too much and had to stop after only about ten yards. Instead, Osborne made his way to the signal box further along the line, in order to raise the alarm. This was a sterling effort as Osborne was unsteady on his feet and had to resort to crawling on hands and knees part of the way.

Unfortunately, by the time the alarm was raised and Osborne and the other railway staff returned, including the signalman and fireman, Kidd was dead. His body was carried to the station waiting room and it was only then, in daylight, that the full horror of the attack became evident: Kidd had been stabbed several times, many of the wounds deep and each struck with great ferocity. The fatal blows had caused a deep gash to the throat, severing both windpipe and artery. Osborne was also badly injured and had lost a great deal of blood. Adrenaline and concern for his colleague had kept him going. Now, with the crisis over, he collapsed unconscious on the floor of the waiting room and was rushed to nearby Wigan Royal Infirmary.

News of the murder was formally reported to Wigan police station, and henceforth this incident was conducted by the Borough Police. Meanwhile, the railway police relayed details of Kidd's murder to his Manchester colleagues, and Mrs Kidd was informed of her husband's brutal murder. She left her home, 17 Zebra Street, Salford and was brought to Wigan by train, for the grim task of formally identifying her husband. When she saw his body she broke down and wept uncontrollably.

A murder inquiry was begun almost immediately and Wigan police were obviously eager to apprehend a suspect for the wilful murder of an officer who they regarded as 'one of their own'. Extensive enquiries were made and the 'usual suspects' were brought in for questioning. The initial focus was on the Scholes area of Wigan, located close to the town centre, run-down and deprived, and noted for its criminal elements. However, drawing a blank there, the police then turned their attention to the neighbouring district of Lower Ince. This too was a deprived area, filled with some of the poorest residents in the town, with a high level of criminality. In particular, information received led the police to concentrate on a row of properties known as 'Kays Houses'. The police mounted a surveillance operation and, once they were satisfied that the suspects were all inside, raided the property during the early hours of Monday 30 September. Their prime suspect, William Kearsley, a local coal miner with a record of theft and assault, was arrested.

Although several other men were apprehended at the same time, they were later released without charge. Two other prime suspects, David Miller and Richard Pritchard, were not inside the house. However, the surveillance operation was maintained on the property and, as luck would have it, both of these men turned up later in the morning and were immediately arrested and taken to the police station. Later that day two more men, James Winstanley and Ralph Brinhall, were also arrested. All the men were remanded in custody and, early the following day, were joined by a sixth suspect, William Halliwell. Within days, yet two more men were arrested, James Whellens and Elijah

Committal proceedings of William Kearsley, Elijah Winstanley and William Halliwell began at Wigan Borough Court, at 10 am on Thursday 10 October 1895.

Winstanley. All of the suspects were subsequently brought before Detective Constable Osborne, still confined to a hospital bed, now conscious and well enough to participate in the identity parade. Although Osborne felt that almost all of the suspects looked familiar, he was more certain when it came to William Kearsley, Elijah Winstanley and William Halliwell. Their identification meant that the others were released without charge and only these three men were brought before Wigan Magistrates' Court.

The case gained great notoriety within Wigan and the surrounding districts, and by the time that the committal proceedings began at Wigan Borough Court, at 10 am on Thursday 10 October 1895, a huge crowd had gathered outside. As the doors opened, scores of people surged forward, all eager to get inside and hear for themselves the case of the murdered detective; however, the court officers were having none of it, and forced the crowd back into the street. The court officers were very selective as to who would be allowed inside and most of the people who had gathered outside that morning were denied admission. In spite of the restrictions, the local and national press were allowed inside, as well as representatives of Wigan's Watch Committee.

As the trial finally got under way, the three accused were formally charged with 'the wilful murder of Detective Sergeant Thomas Kidd, and the assault, inflicting actual bodily harm upon Detective Constable William Henry Osborne, while in the execution of their duty, at the goods yard of the London & North Western Railway at Wigan on Sunday 29 September 1895'.

Of the three accused, only William Halliwell had acquired the services of a defence barrister, a Mr Lees. This decision would prove decisive in the case, as Lees immediately entered into negotiations with the prosecution and succeeded in having the main charge of murder withdrawn from his client – providing he would appear as a prosecution witness against both Kearsley and Winstanley, who were half-brothers. Although the charge of actual bodily harm against DC Osborne still stood, this would be heard at a later date and Halliwell was free to leave the dock. However, as he was escorted into open court there was uproar, Elijah Winstanley losing all self control, exclaiming loudly: 'I did it, I did it. But I did not intend to kill him. I did it, not our Bill. So kill me, kill me!'

Once order was restored, the prosecution began to lay out their case, led by Mr Kershaw, a London-based barrister who had travelled to Wigan especially for the trial. The prosecution felt that they had compelling evidence against Elijah Winstanley whose right hand, and in particular his thumb, was badly bruised. DC Osborne had confirmed that he had struck one of his attackers on the hand with his truncheon during the fight. Also, bloodstained clothing and clogs had been retrieved from Winstanley's home by the police. During the line-up at Wigan Infirmary DC Osborne had clearly identified Winstanley as 'very like one of the men at the scene of the murder'.

Halliwell, now a witness for the prosecution, provided an account of the events of 29 September that would implicate both Winstanley and Kearsley in the detective's murder. He claimed that he had known both of the accused for many years and had accompanied them on an early evening pub crawl. After spending some time in the *New Inn* at Lower Ince, they went to the *Fox Tavern* in Chapel Lane and decided to climb the fence surrounding the railway goods yard. Halliwell claimed that he acted as a look-out, while Kearsley and Winstanley attempted to break into one of the stationary wagons. Before the two men could gain entry to the wagon the police were upon them. Halliwell said that he recalled struggling with an officer, and somehow managing to take his truncheon, and vividly recalled striking him about the head with it and kicking him several times before running away. He then told the court that he then went into the *Fox Tavern* where he was later joined by both Winstanley and Kearsley.

At this point Mr Kershaw intervened, asking him if both Winstanley and Kearsley were still wearing the same clothes as before. Halliwell confirmed that they were, except that they were missing their caps. A number of flat cloth caps had been retrieved from the murder scene, and when these were now shown to Halliwell he confirmed one of them as 'belonging to Winstanley'.

Halliwell recalled the conversation he had with the two accused in the *Fox Tavern*, saying that Winstanley had told him that in order to escape he had stabbed the other officer 'several times' before getting away. With this damning evidence, both Winstanley and Kearsley were committed to stand trial at the Liverpool Assizes, and both men would be held at Walton Prison on remand.

A coroner's inquest was held at the Borough Police Court on Thursday 17 October, to investigate the circumstances surrounding the death while on duty of Detective Sergeant Robert Kidd. Dr Graham, who had conducted the post-mortem, confirmed that Robert Kidd was stabbed a total of nine times by a thin-bladed knife. Other wounds included 'defensive injuries' – punctures to the hands; and the index finger of the left hand had been completely severed. Of the nine main wounds, the three to the neck had proved fatal, severing an artery, and allowing DS Kidd to 'bleed to death'.

Despite being offered the opportunity to attend court, Kearsley and Winstanley declined, though Halliwell accepted and his evidence was to prove crucial. At first he began by simply repeating his testimony from the committal proceedings, though at the end he added something new. Halliwell now said that Winstanley had told him that his half-brother, William Kearsley, had held the officer down while he stabbed him. When challenged, Halliwell said that Winstanley had said: 'I don't think the man I was "agate" [engaged or fought] with could live because I stabbed him many a time, while our Bill holded him.' This was damning stuff and, despite Winstanley's utterances to the contrary during the committal proceedings, it clearly implicated Kearsley in Kidd's murder. The jury in the coroner's court had little option but to present a verdict of 'wilful murder', concluding that 'Detective Sergeant Kidd met his death in the discharge of his duty . . . at the hands of Elijah Winstanley and William Kearsley'.

The trial of William Kearsley, Elijah Winstanley and William Halliwell began at Liverpool Assizes on Tuesday 26 November before Justice Henn Collins. Although the main count was the wilful murder of DS Kidd by Winstanley and Kearsley, Halliwell was charged with actual bodily harm upon DC Osborne; and all three had the additional charges of trespass and theft from L&NWR property. Pleas of not guilty were presented from all three men to all charges. During the committal proceedings only Halliwell had been represented by a barrister, though on this occasion all three men had legal representation. Kearsley was represented by Mr McKeand, Winstanley by Mr Cottingham, and Halliwell by Mr Ambrose-Jones. By now all three men were suffering the strain of the build-up to the trial, looking drawn and haggard, and Halliwell actually collapsed in the witness box while giving evidence.

For the prosecution, Mr Kershaw was joined by a Mr Pickford QC. Since the committal proceedings, the murder weapon, a heavily bloodstained, thin-bladed penknife with a white bone handle, had been discovered on wasteland alongside the railway by Joseph Glover, a local iron-roller, on 3 November, and handed in to the police. Mr Kershaw informed the court that several people had confirmed that this knife was 'very much like' one owned by Winstanley, and if needs be, witnesses could be called to support this statement. The defence did not contest the prosecution's claim, however. The amount of evidence against Winstanley was such that there was little Cottingham could offer against it. He did, however, ask Halliwell whether Winstanley had told him that he had stabbed the officer only in self-defence, though Halliwell said that the words 'in self-defence' had never been mentioned.

The case against William Kearsley was less certain. The prosecution only had the word of Halliwell, a known felon who was also charged with the assault upon DC Osborne; and McKeard urged the jury to give him the benefit of doubt. However, during his summing up, Justice Collins advised the jury that anyone assisting in the attack upon DS Kidd, whether he struck the fatal blow or not, was equally guilty of murder.

The jury declined to retire and, after just fifteen minutes' deliberation delivered their verdict, finding both men guilty of the wilful murder of DS Kidd while in the execution of his duty. When asked if they had anything to say to the court, Kearsley maintained his innocence, saying simply: 'I didn't do it.' Winstanley supported his half-brother when he said: 'It was me as did it . . . our Bill never touched him . . . and that's God's truth. Halliwell tells lies.' Justice Collins seemed unmoved by these statements and, donning his black cap, passed the sentence of death on both men.

The following day, William Halliwell returned to stand in the dock, accused of actual bodily harm on DC Osborne. He had been assured by both the police and the prosecution that if he gave evidence against both Kearsley and Winstanley for the murder of DS Kidd he would go free. They remained true to their word and, with no case to answer, Halliwell walked out of Liverpool Assizes a free man.

The news that the death sentence had been passed on both Winstanley and Kearsley shocked many people in Wigan and a petition began almost immediately, gaining a great many signatures. In the meantime, the respective defence counsels for both men appealed direct to the Home Secretary for his intervention in this case. The intended execution, scheduled for Tuesday 3 December at Walton Prison, was delayed while the Home Secretary reviewed the case notes and reached a decision. The Home Secretary concluded that it was clear that Elijah Winstanley was the man who stabbed DS Kidd, and was therefore guilty of wilful murder, so his appeal was rejected. However, the role played by his half-brother, William Kearsley, was less certain. So, under the circumstances, he decided to grant his appeal, commuting his sentence to a term of penal servitude.

Elijah Winstanley, a thirty-two-year-old coal miner from Lower Ince, Wigan, was hanged in Walton Prison at 8 am on Tuesday 17 December 1895, for the murder of Robert Kidd. His accomplice and half-brother, William Kearsley, was released from prison on 7 February 1903, after serving just seven years.

CHAPTER 14

Incest & Murder

1896

John Green was lying on his back in a pool of blood . . .

The circumstances surrounding the murder of John Green were complicated. Green's attacker was his brother-in-law, John Vaughan; the two men having become related when they married sisters. Since Green's wife had died some fifteen years earlier, he and his children had been living with the Vaughan family in their house on Bolton Street, Scholes. The extended family seemed to be getting on well, or perhaps too well, when in early 1896 Green's daughter, Mary Ellen, who had been just two years old when her mother had died and was now seventeen, discovered she was pregnant and, to the family's great surprise, alleged that her uncle was the father.

The allegation of incest divided the family and caused John Green and his children to move out, renting a house at 3 William Street, Wigan. Vaughan denied having improper relations with his niece, and said that the child could not be his. The matter was officially resolved in the local courts during the spring of 1896. The conclusion was that the child was Vaughan's and he was ordered to pay maintenance; but the situation continued to cause great anger and resentment between the two men.

John Green returned to Bolton Street on Saturday 2 May to collect some of his belongings. He had been drinking for much of the day and when he arrived at the Vaughan household around 5.30 pm he was heavily intoxicated. He found the door ajar and, although he called out several times, there was no reply. Green entered the house and proceeded to collect his belongings which, since his absence, had been stored in the washhouse. What exactly happened once John Green was inside the property is not known. Several of the Bolton Street residents saw him enter, and many of them also saw Vaughan leave the house a few minutes later, looking in a disturbed state.

John Green rented a house in William Street.

One of the witnesses was a young lad who, having seen Green enter the house and Vaughan leave in a hurry, thought it was suspicious and said this to Mrs Vaughan who came walking up Bolton Street a few minutes later.

Mrs Vaughan, accompanied by her lodger, Joseph Barker, entered the house but found nothing untoward. In the meantime, word of 'something going on' had circulated the neighbourhood and the curiosity of a local young lad had got the better of him and caused him to go down the alleyway that ran the length of the rear of the terraced row to look through the gate and into the Vaughans' backyard. What he saw shocked him so much that he immediately ran home to fetch his father, William Gaskell. The two of them returned soon after and, making sure his son remained in the alleyway, William Gaskell climbed over the wall and into the Vaughans' yard. John Green was lying on his back in a pool of blood; his face had been disfigured by several blows from something sharp and heavy. Not only was John Green still alive, but he was conscious and in severe pain. Gaskell summoned assistance from the other neighbours who, by now, had gathered in a large group in the alleyway. They brought water, towels and bandages, and Gaskell did his best to attend to Green's wounds, before they carried the badly injured man to his own house a few streets away. Although Green had been conscious and talking while Gaskell had been with him in the yard, by the time they reached William Street he had slipped into unconsciousness.

The police were summoned by the neighbours and arrived on the scene around 6.30 pm. They discovered that, in the time it had taken to carry John Green to his home on William Street, someone had gone to great pains to clean up the backyard. When questioned by police, William Gaskell would describe the backyard he saw as covered in blood, with three large pools of blood on the floor and blood splatter on the walls and the gate. When the police inspected the yard the blood splatter had been wiped clean and the pools of blood had been covered with ashes.

John Vaughan was the prime suspect and a warrant was issued for his arrest. The immediate area around Bolton Street was searched, but he was nowhere to be seen. Vaughan was

John Vaughan, the prime suspect for the murder of John Green, was arrested in Standish and taken to King Street police station for questioning.

Wigan Infirmary, c1800s. John Green was admitted to Wigan Infirmary on 4 May but, despite the best efforts of the nursing staff, he died there five days later.

finally arrested in Standish early the following morning and taken to King Street police station, and later appeared before the Wigan Police Court, charged with assault and grievous bodily harm.

John Green was attended to in his own home until he was admitted to Wigan Infirmary on Monday 4 May. Nevertheless, despite the best efforts of the hospital staff, he never regained consciousness and died from his wounds on Saturday 9 May – exactly a week since he had been savagely attacked. The police immediately altered the charge against Vaughan to one of murder.

An inquest was convened by Mr Millington, Deputy Borough Coroner, on the afternoon of Wednesday 13 May in the Borough Police Courts. The prosecution was led by Mr Wilson, and the defence by Mr Smith. Several witnesses were summoned to give evidence. Dr Monks and Dr Milroy, who had carried out the port-mortem on John Green the day before, concluded that he had died as a result of a blow to the head by a heavy and sharp metal instrument which had caused a 'serious fracture to the skull . . . extending some twelve inches'. As a hatchet had been recovered from the murder scene, Dr Monks was asked whether that could have been used in the assault, and he informed the coroner that such an instrument could well have been the murder weapon. However, there was a serious problem with this assumption, as the police later informed the coroner that the hatchet recovered from Vaughan's yard was clean, and not only did it not contain any bloodstains, but in their opinion, it did not appear as though it had been cleaned recently. PC Brooks, who had arrested John Vaughan at Standish on 5 May, informed the court that the prisoner when challenged had said: 'I never did it . . . I did not strike him on the head, I caught him with my fist across his jaw and knocked him against the wall because he called me a pauper.'

Several witnesses came forward to confirm the awkward relationship between the two men, including James Green, son of the deceased and nephew of the accused, who explained how the two men had fallen out over his sister's pregnancy. Other witnesses, residents of Bolton Street, including Thomas Long, confirmed that John Green had entered the house and shortly after, John Vaughan had left the house in what was referred to as an 'odd state'. Another witness, Mary Barton, had seen Vaughan soon after he had left his home and he simply brushed past her without either acknowledging her or speaking to her, which she described as unusual behaviour. The jury returned a verdict of wilful murder, and John Vaughan was committed to appear before the next Liverpool Assizes.

John Vaughan, referred to as a common labourer from Wigan, appeared before Justice Kaye at the Liverpool Assizes on Saturday 1 August 1896. He was charged with the wilful murder of John Green, a collier from Wigan, to which he pleaded not guilty. The prosecution's case, led by Mr Cottingham, hinged on the fact that the two men had quarrelled and that Vaughan had struck Green over the head with the hatchet. The defence counsel, led by Mr McKeever, exploited the fact that their client had not denied arguing with John Green in the yard, and admitted to punching him in the face, causing him to stumble backwards, banging his head on the wall as he fell. John Vaughan denied striking his brother-in-law with the hatchet, and Mr McKeever drove a coach and horses through the prosecution case by informing the jury that, despite careful forensic examination of the hatchet recovered by police from the yard, they had found no traces of blood on it. Mr Keever asked the jury to consider the facts, and pointed out that if the hatchet had been used and then wiped clean, then where was the bloodstained cloth? And if the murderer had removed the cloth, then why not simply remove the hatchet instead? McKeever pointed out that there was insufficient evidence to convict John Vaughan of murder, and the lesser verdict of manslaughter would be more fitting.

The jury, who had listened intently to all the evidence and the emotive closing argument from both counsels, did not leave the court, but instead deliberated for only a few moments before returning a verdict of manslaughter against John Vaughan. Justice Kaye informed Vaughan that, in light of the lack of evidence to exactly what had occurred between him and the deceased in the yard that evening in May, a murder verdict had not been returned. Nevertheless, causing the death of a man by punching him was still grave act, and the verdict of manslaughter in such a case deserved a severe sentence. However, taking his age into account he sentenced Vaughan to sixteen years in prison. John Vaughan, who was fifty-eight, had in effect been given a life sentence, and died in prison.

CHAPTER 15

The Wasteful Wife

1899

I have been driven to do what I have done through poverty and misery

Domestic violence and murder was common in working-class towns, like Wigan, and particularly during the Victorian era. However, the vast majority of cases were young married couples and often the situation was fuelled by alcohol. What's different about the murder of Margaret Tighe by her husband, Martin, was that they were in late middle-age and although the victim had been drinking, the attacker had not.

The couple, who lived at 90 Great George Street, had been married for almost thirty-four years and had raised nine children. Martin was sixty-one and had been a pit sinker all his working life, until an industrial accident in 1894 rendered him unable to work. Since then life had become a great deal more difficult for the family, their income drastically reduced. Matters were made all the worse by the fact that Mrs Tighe had a serious drink problem, often squandering all of the house-keeping on alcohol rather than putting food on the table. This, and the family's financial insecurity, had created tension in an otherwise happy marriage. Although five of the older children had left home, the three younger children (the youngest being just four years old) were still at home. Their eldest child, nineteen-year-old Agnes, was as yet unmarried and had remained at home; in many ways it was a good job she had, as her meagre wages from working at nearby Trencherfield Mill was a welcome boost to the family purse.

The day of the murder, Monday 10 July 1899, was in many ways just like any other. Both Mr and Mrs Tighe had spent the day inside. When a neighbour, Elizabeth Walsh, called by at 4.30 pm, she found them both sitting by the fireside, chatting and talking. The mood changed later when Margaret decided to nip to the local public house for several pints of beer, which she

Number 90 Great George Street, the former home of the Tighe family, no longer exists. All of the slum terraced houses that once inhabited Great George Street were demolished and the area redeveloped and designated as an 'industrial sector'.

bought back to the house and shared with her friend. Martin, who had not moved from his chair by the fireside, was less than pleased. He scolded his wife for squandering 15s 6d, what little money they had, on ale, when it could have been used more productively; he pointed out that it could have bought 'oatmeal and milk'. Margaret dismissed his criticism, though she added that once Agnes came home from work she could nip to the local shop for his oatmeal and milk. Martin was not amused by his wife's carefree attitude, and was less than satisfied with her promise. An argument erupted, but soon name calling and general abuse escalated into violence, when Martin jumped up from his chair and, grabbing his wife by the arm, he threw her to the floor.

The scuffle ended when Elizabeth Walsh scolded Mr Tighe for ill-treating his wife in this way. Seeing that there was much bad feeling between the couple, Elizabeth Walsh remained in the Tighe house until their daughter, Agnes, came in from work. The quarrelling pair continued to argue, but there was no

Wigan Pier, on the Leeds & Liverpool Canal, with Trencherfield Mill, where Agnes Tighe worked, standing in the background.

more violence. Later that evening, Martin Tighe was still complaining about not getting his oatmeal and milk, so at about 7 pm he gave his daughter a few coppers and sent her out to get some, leaving him and his wife alone. Although Agnes was only gone a matter of minutes, when she returned she found the door locked. Although she banged on the door and shouted for someone to let her inside there was no response. Frustrated and concerned, she began to kick at the door, violently breaking a panel; and it was only then that her father unlocked it and let her inside.

Agnes followed her father inside the house, though the scene that confronted her was something she could never have imagined: her mother lay dead on the kitchen floor and a pool of bright red blood had gathered around her body. Agnes was horrified and, realising that her mother was dead, she screamed at her father: 'What have you done?' before running out into the street screaming: 'Murder! Murder! My mother's dead!'

Many of the neighbours heard her screams, including James Walker from No 83 and James Shawcross from No 81. Both men ran into the house. Mr Walker felt for a pulse, but Mrs Tighe appeared to be dead. Mr Shawcross ran to fetch a doctor. Walker challenged Mr Tighe, asking: 'What have you been doing Tighe? She's dead.' The only reply that Mr Tighe gave was to say that he knew his wife was dead, and that he should have murdered her years ago. Walker later recalled two large carving knives on the kitchen table, each covered in blood.

Mr Shawcross returned soon after, accompanied by PC Newcombe, who confirmed that Mrs Tighe was deceased. Mr Walker handed the officer the two bloodstained knives from the kitchen table. Dr Aldred, the Deputy Police Surgeon, was the next to arrive on the scene, followed soon after by Police Superintendent Earnshaw and Police Inspector Fowler. The crime had aroused so much interest that even Mr Hardy, the Chief Constable turned up at the house later on. In the meantime, Mr Tighe was placed under arrest and escorted to King Street police station where he was formally charged with the murder of his wife. He appeared before the Wigan magistrates' court the following morning, where he was remanded into custody pending trial.

Mr Tighe was placed under arrest and escorted to King Street police station where he was formally charged with the murder of his wife.

Mrs Tighe's body was taken to the borough mortuary where it underwent a post-mortem examination by Dr Aldred. He found that Mrs Tighe had been stabbed repeatedly. He later confirmed that there were 'incised wounds on the abdomen, vertical incised wounds on the left of the neck, and incised wounds on the front of the neck'. Dr Aldred also found that there were further 'incised wounds on the hands, evidently received by the deceased women attempting to ward off the blows'. In total, Mrs Tighe had suffered twenty-six separate stab wounds.

We gain an insight into the murder scene from a correspondent from the *Wigan Observer* who visited the crime scene later that evening. He described the Tighe family home, which was situated about halfway down Great George Street on the left hand side, as being 'very dismal and foreboding in appearance, the structures on either side being grimy and black with smoke'. He added that the inhabitants of such a street were 'working classes whose life is a miserable existence of hand-to-mouth'. Once inside, the correspondent described the kitchen floor as 'swimming with blood' and said that the sheet of newspaper which had been used as a makeshift tablecloth for the kitchen table 'bore dark traces of the heavily bloodstained knives which had been placed upon it'.

An inquest was held, led by the County Coroner, Mr Billingham. The two knives which had been taken from the house had now been forensically examined and police confirmed that they were the murder weapons. Dr Aldred, the police surgeon, informed the court that Margaret Tighe had been stabbed twenty-six times, each blow had been struck with a great deal of force, and penetrated the torso right up to the hilt. In the course of what could be described as a frenzied attack, several major arteries had been severed making death almost instantaneous.

Several witnesses were called, including Elizabeth Walsh, who recounted the events of the afternoon and the quarrel that erupted between Mr and Mrs Tighe. The couple's eldest child, Agnes, also took the witness stand and, when asked about her parents' relationship prior to her mother's death, told the court that her mother and father had once been very happy, though things had gone bad since her father had lost his job some five years ago. Since then he had given up on life and become lazy and uncaring. Moreover, she explained that her mother had deteriorated mentally and had turned to the drink, spending what little money the family had on alcohol. When she had no money she would take items to the local pawnshop. Agnes elaborated, pointing out that despite the fact that there were three adults and three young children living under one roof, there wasn't a single bed in the house, as her mother had taken them all to the pawn! On the day of the murder, Agnes told the court that she had returned from work to find no food in the house. Mr Billington enquired as to whether Mr Tighe had been a good father to her and her brother and sisters, and Agnes confirmed that he had. The jury found Martin Tighe guilty of murdering his wife and the case was referred to the next Liverpool Assizes.

Martin Tighe appeared before Justice Wills at the Liverpool Assizes on Tuesday 2 August 1899, charged with the wilful murder of his wife, Margaret Tighe. He entered a plea of not guilty. For the prosecuting counsel, led by Mr Tobin, Martin Tighe was a cold blooded murderer. There were no mitigating circumstances behind the crime; Tighe had attacked his wife with two separate knives, stabbing her repeatedly. And, even though the prosecution suggested that Mrs Tighe had pleaded for her life on the grounds that there were clear defensive wounds inflicted to her hands, her husband had continued this frenzied attack. The defence, led by Mr Rigby-Smith, called for a manslaughter verdict on the grounds that there was clear provocation for the attack. Mrs Tighe was a drunkard, who had pawned almost all of the family's possessions to buy alcohol and had nagged her husband to the point where he could no longer take it. The defence agreed that it was a frenzied attack, but that surely pointed to the fact that Mr Tighe was not in full control of his mind when he carried it out. Mr Justice Wills seemed to have been swayed by the passionate plea from the defence counsel, though during his summing up of the case he pointed out to the jury that for such an unprovoked attack which had resulted in the horrific death of Mrs Tighe there could be no other possible verdict but murder. However, taking into account the pressure and strain that the accused had been under, Mr Justice Wills did reiterate Martin Tighe's explanation to the jury prior to their verdict: 'I have been driven to do what I have done through poverty and misery.'

The jury took only a matter of minutes to reach their verdict and seemed moved by the circumstances of the case. Although they returned a verdict of guilty against Martin Tighe, they also added that mercy should be shown. In passing the death sentence, Mr Justice Wills took the jury's mercy plea into account, and recommended that the matter should be passed to the Home Secretary with the greatest urgency. The Home Secretary did indeed review the case and found that there was some mitigation and changed the sentence to life imprisonment.

CHAPTER 16

The Body in the Canal

1900

He jumped in the canal . . . but was unable to save her

Despite high expectations, the early years of the new century would witness little change and even less improvement in the lives of the common population: in 1900 crime, especially murder, particularly amongst the poor working class was still as common as ever.

The relationship between Ellen Jeffries and William Wood seemed doomed from the start. The couple met before the New Year and like many, wished it was to be a good year for them. In actual fact they could not have been more wrong, as Ellen was soon to fall pregnant, putting great strain on their fledgling relationship. William, a collier, did the honourable thing and agreed to marry her. The wedding was hastily arranged and the couple became man and wife on 14 February.

It was not to be a happy marriage. They were both in their early twenties and neither of them was on a large income. William was not a grafter and his frequent absences from the pit limited his income. Ellen was employed at the *Victoria Hotel* as a laundress which was a low-paid job. Times were hard and this made their relationship almost impossible. By the time that Ellen gave birth to their daughter, the marriage was showing signs of strain, and the couple separated at Christmas 1899. Although Ellen returned to her family home, where her mother assisted in bringing up her child, William kept on seeing her and eventually she took him back. The couple lodged with her mother, Mrs Jeffries, but it was not to last. The final straw came in March 1900, when Ellen became suspicious that her husband was seeing other women, and they separated. Ellen returned to working at the *Victoria Hotel*, living there, while her daughter remained with Mrs Jeffries. Meanwhile, William gave up the house they had been renting together and moved into lodgings.

Although the couple were parted for a while, William found

Ellen Jeffries worked at the *Victoria Hotel* on Wallgate as a laundress.

that he missed his wife and he was the first to attempt to rekindle their relationship. He began seeing his Ellen, meeting her from work and, while her mother took care of the child, the couple would walk out together. This situation continued for some time. Both of them seemed content to continue seeing one another, though they continued to live apart and neither suggested living together again, at least at this stage in their 'new' relationship. William would meet his wife from work and soon became a regular visitor to the hotel and the staff accepted him.

On Monday 17 September, William met his wife outside the hotel as usual at around 7 pm, and they went for a walk together. Staff would recall that Ellen returned to the hotel around 8.30 pm, but went out again soon after. Witnesses would later recall seeing her walking down Wallgate in the direction of the canal.

When Ellen did not arrive for work the following day, the staff did not think too much of it. After all, for a young mother there could be several legitimate reasons why she had not reported for work: perhaps she was ill, or maybe the baby was sickly. When she failed to report for work on the Wednesday morning they became more concerned. Later that day, William Wood turned up at the rear of the *Victoria Hotel* and informed the staff that Ellen had decided to hand in her notice as she was moving back in with him. He asked them to gather up her belongings and any money that was due to his wife and he would collect it by the end of the week. Wood was told that although he could have his wife's clothes and other items, any money that she might be due could only be paid directly to his wife and not him.

Late on Wednesday evening, a man rushed into King Street police station saying that a woman's body was floating in the Leeds & Liverpool Canal alongside the Pagefield Ironworks. PC McFay attended the scene and found the woman's body stuck fast in the mud and silt gathered on the canal bed. Gaining assistance, he managed to free the body and drag it to

On the afternoon of Wednesday 19 October, William Wood turned up at the rear of the *Victoria Hotel* and informed the staff that Ellen had decided to hand in her notice as she was moving back in with him, and asked them to gather up her belongings and any money that was due to his wife and he would collect it by the end of the week.

Late on the evening of Wednesday 19 October 1900, a man rushed into King Street police station saying that a woman's body was floating in the Leeds & Liverpool Canal alongside the Pagefield Ironworks.

the towpath. The corpse, which bore no form of identification, was taken to Wigan mortuary.

By the following day, Thursday 20 September, news of 'the body in the canal' had circulated around the town, and the staff of the *Victoria Hotel* had become concerned that it may be linked to Ellen's sudden disappearance. Enquiring at the police station, they were told that a hat had been found floating in the canal a little further down from where the woman's body had been hauled out. When the police showed this hat to Ellen's former workmates they all identified it as belonging to Mrs Wood. They were subsequently taken to the mortuary and formally identified the body as that of Ellen Wood.

When the police were told that Ellen Wood had last been seen with her estranged husband, William Wood, on Wednesday evening walking in the direction of the canal, and that he had since come around to the hotel asking for her belongings and wages, he became the prime suspect and a warrant was issued for his arrest. Later that same evening, William Wood would be arrested alongside the Leeds & Liverpool Canal close to the point where his wife's body had been found two days before. He was taken to King Street police station and questioned. Wood claimed that he and his wife had

William Wood was arrested and taken to King Street police station. Today Wigan's modern police station is situated at Scholes.

been walking along the canal towpath, a popular venue for lovers, and that she had accidentally slipped into the water. He had immediately jumped in the canal after her, but had been unable to save her. He told police that he panicked and, rather than summoning assistance, or even reporting the accident to the police, he simply went home. The police were far from convinced.

An inquest was convened by the Deputy Borough Coroner, Mr Millington, at Wigan Borough Courts on Thursday 27 September 1900. Wood was represented by Mr Shawcross. Several witnesses gave evidence to the court, including Mrs Jeffries, who provided background information to the poor relationship which her daughter had experienced with William Wood. Eleanor Pender, laundress at the *Victoria Hotel*, and former friend of the deceased, also gave evidence. She told the court that she had been around when William Wood had collected his wife on the Monday evening, and she said that the couple appeared happy in each other's company. She had also been the member of staff which Wood had spoken to on the Wednesday evening when he enquired about Ellen's belongings and wages. She had asked Wood where Ellen was and he had told her that she had gone to Lowton, a village located between Wigan and Warrington.

William Wood maintained his innocence throughout, and stuck to the story which he had told to the police following his arrest, claiming that Ellen had fallen into the canal and that try as he might he was unable to save her. James Wood also gave evidence, corroborating his brother's statement, informing the court that on the night of the murder, Wednesday 19 September, William had turned up at his house on Canal Street soaking wet, claiming he had fallen into the canal.

PC McFay, who had extracted Ellen Wood's body from the Leeds & Liverpool Canal, told the deputy coroner that she had been stuck fast in the mud and he and others had struggled to free her before they could get the body to the canal bank. He went on to add that once on the tow path, although the body was very dirty, which was understandable, there were no obvious or noticeable marks to suggest that she had been attacked prior to going into the water. The Police Surgeon, Dr Roocroft, who had examined the body at the mortuary and later performed an autopsy, informed the deputy coroner that he had found a contusion to the woman's head. When asked by Mr Millington 'had this occurred before or after death?' Dr

James Wood corroborated his brother's statement, saying that on the night of Wednesday 19 September, William had turned up at his house on Canal Street soaking wet, claiming he had fallen into the canal. Canal Street still survives today though James Wood's house has long since been demolished and now the street is home to several industrial units.

Roocroft confirmed that it had definitely occurred before death, though he could not determine whether it had happened before or after entering the canal.

William Wood appeared in the court well-dressed, wearing a suit and tie, and although he had remained quiet, he looked alert and appeared to be following the proceedings. However, when he was called to give evidence, he seemed confused and began to mumble his words, in fact his speech became so incoherent that he was eventually excused from testifying. Mr Millington, the deputy coroner, summed up the evidence, such as it was, and asked the jury to consider their verdict. The jury found William Wood guilty of the murder of his wife, and he was remanded to the Liverpool Assizes.

Appearing before Justice Danby on 5 December 1900, William Wood entered a plea of 'not guilty'. The prosecution, led by Mr McKeand and Mr Steele, began their case by going over the facts, informing the jury of how the couple had met, and how Wood had been forced to marry Ellen after she had fallen pregnant. They laboured the point that this had never been a happy marriage, and how, in their opinion, Wood despised his wife, inferring that he had only begun seeing her again with the full intention of murdering her. They brought into question Wood's character, pointing out that, if as Wood had claimed, Ellen had accidentally fallen into the canal why had he not tried harder to save her. McKeand said he was confused, as he could not understand why Wood had not sought his brother's assistance, after all Canal Street was only a few hundred yards from where Ellen had supposedly fallen in. McKeand pointed out to the jury that after arriving on his brother's doorstep soaking wet he never mentioned that his wife was lying in the canal. The prosecution also suggested that Wood was much more interested in getting his hands on the wages which his wife was owed, after all that was why he had gone around to the *Victoria Hotel* two days after the murder. Several of Ellen's former workmates were called as witnesses for the prosecution, such as chambermaid Alice Jolley, who told the court that Wood and Ellen often fought over money. Ellen's brother, Joseph, also gave evidence that Wood had threatened his sister on several occasions.

Defence counsel, led by Mr Shawcross and Mr McKeever, maintained Wood's story that Ellen had fallen into the canal by accident. They dismissed the prosecution's calls on Wood's character, pointing out that the accused was being tried for murder, not cowardice. McKeever also pointed out to the jury that, in the absence of any eyewitnesses to the events on the canal, the evidence against their client was circumstantial at best, and that he could not and should not be held responsible for what had been a terrible accident. They explained the contusion to Ellen's head as being inflicted while she was in the water, as canals were notorious dumping grounds for a variety of rubbish.

Justice Danby summed up the case by saying to the jury that they should not judge William Wood on his character but simply on whether Ellen Wood had died as a result of a terrible accident or by malicious intent. The jury retired to consider their verdict, though returned to the court room within the hour. Although they found William Wood guilty of the murder of his wife they included a recommendation that the judge be merciful towards him when passing sentence. Despite such a recommendation, Justice Danby passed the death sentence on Wood. The case had aroused great passion within Wigan and a sizable petition was sent to the Home Secretary, who taking it and the jury's recommendation for mercy into account, commuted Wood's sentence to life imprisonment.

CHAPTER 17

The Highwayman's Haunt

1786 & 1904

George Lyon's poltergeist . . .

The village of Up Holland, on the outskirts of Wigan, has a long and varied history. Through the years the place has had a variety of owners, though the most famous and clearly the most influential were the De Hollands. Matthew de Holland was awarded land here following the Conquest and his family shaped the destiny of Up Holland for many years.

The De Hollands' influence stretched far and wide. For instance, Matthew's grandson, Robert, later became Baron De Holland, and his son, Thomas, became the Earl of Kent following his marriage to Joan, granddaughter of Edward I. However, it was the ruthless character of Sir Robert De Holland, right-hand man to Thomas, Earl of Lancaster which would be the family's undoing, resulting in the Banastre

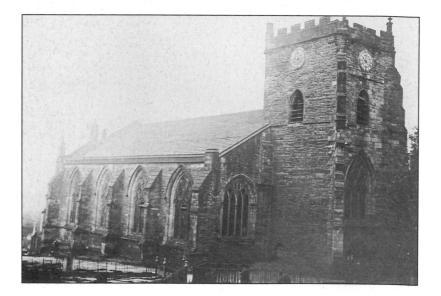

This page and opposite:
Sir Robert De Holland built Up Holland Priory in 1317. It played an important role in the religious affairs of the region until its partial demolition during the Dissolution when only the priory church survived. The only surviving remnant of the original priory is a short section of wall containing an upper section of an archway seen in the car park of the Up Holland Conservative Club (the former vicarage).

The Stanley family, earls of Derby, owned Up Holland for a time and their former manor house still stands on School Lane, bearing the famous 'eagle & child' crest which the family inherited from the Lathoms by marriage.

Rebellion in 1315. And yet just two years later that same Sir Robert built Up Holland Priory, dedicated to St Thomas. The Priory was demolished following the Dissolution, though parts survived as a priory church.

Following the defeat of Richard III, the manor of Up Holland was inherited by the most influential of all the Lancashire families, the Stanleys, Earls of Derby. The Stanley family would attain so much power and influence that they were often referred to as 'Kings of Lancashire'. Their manor house still exists on School Lane.

The English Civil War would be the undoing of the Stanley family. By the middle of the seventeenth century they had sold Up Holland, and the manor passed through a variety of owners.

By the eighteenth century, Up Holland had gained a much more sinister reputation, becoming the favoured haunt of the area's much feared and despised highwaymen. As the nation's highways had begun to improve with the creation of the turnpikes, a network of stagecoaches had been established connecting the major towns and cities with regular services. These stages, often carrying wealthy passengers – merchants, bankers, solicitors and other professionals – had become the easy pickings of robbers and thieves. Highway robbery was a lucrative trade, and the daring highwayman could gather vast funds in a relatively short period of time. Despite increasing efforts by the authorities to dissuade and curtail their activities, the highwaymen continued their despicable trade and bred fear into the hearts of the traveller.

Highwaymen became legends in their own lifetimes. Although the daring exploits of ruthless men like Dick Turpin gained national notoriety, within south Lancashire the most famous highwayman was George Lyon. The *White Lion* public house at Up Holland, located opposite the old priory, gained a reputation as being a den of villains and cut-throats, as it became the favoured meeting place of Lyon and his associates, including David Bennett and William Houghton.

Born in 1761, young George Lyon, like many of his contemporaries, had a meagre education. He later trained as a handloom weaver. The introduction of labour-saving devices, like the flying shuttle and the power-loom, brought a decline to the once lucrative trade; and many handloom weavers faced unemployment and starvation. Whether it was this prospect that drove George Lyon to a life of crime is mere speculation. Many considered Lyon to be a latter-day Robin Hood,

This page and opposite:
Historic Up Holland gained a more sinister reputation during the late eighteenth and early nineteenth centuries as a safe haven for criminals, and in particular highwaymen who prowled the roads and highways in the region preying on unsuspecting victims.

stealing from the rich to feed the poor. Although many stories are told of how he distributed stolen bread to the needy families in the village, it's questionable as to whether Lyon was a philanthropist.

Lyon and his associates held up the stagecoach at Tawd Bridge. He was eventually arrested during April 1786 for the robbery of Robert Smith of Winstanley on the 'King's Highway within the Parish of Wigan'. He appeared before Judge Edward Willies at Lancaster Assizes, where he was sentenced to seven years' transportation, to the colonies. Twenty-five years old, Lyon must have been shocked by his short stay within the Lancaster Gaol, with its fearsome reputation, and his time within the Americas. Yet when he arrived back home he simply took up where he had left off, immediately returning to criminality.

By this time, Up Holland had gained the dubious reputation of a safe haven for villains, almost becoming a 'no go area' for the authorities. The village was so safe that Lyon, with a substantial price on his head, felt safe and secure enough to lodge in a house on Church Street, next door to the *White Lion* public house. Nevertheless, by the end of the eighteenth century, travellers and the stage coaches' companies had grown

The *White Lion* public house became a den of villains and cut-throats, and the favoured meeting place of highwaymen like George Lyon, David Bennett and William Houghton.

increasingly weary of the relentless activities of the highwaymen and, as the new century dawned, the authorities had begun to come down hard. Many highwaymen were captured and executed.

Such a fate was in store for George Lyon. One of his last exploits was to break into Westwood Hall, at Ince, accompanied by Bennett and Houghton, stealing a quantity of silver. John Cooper, Wigan's Chief Constable, had been unable to plant any informers into Lyon's gang of cut-throats, so he called on the resources of Joseph Nadin, Deputy Constable of Manchester, who sent in John MacDonald undercover to infiltrate the criminal gang. Despite Lyon's initial scepticism and suspicion of MacDonald, he offered to meet with him at the *Bull's Head,* on 10 October 1814 – in order to sell him a 'load of silver'. This rendezvous provided the authorities with sufficient evidence, and Lyon was subsequently arrested at his home and taken to Wigan where he was charged before John Cooper. He was subsequently tried at Lancaster Assizes and, having been found guilty of his many crimes, including highway robbery and 'burglary by force', was sentenced to death and hanged in Lancaster Castle's infamous Drop Room, on Saturday 22 April 1815. Lyon's body was returned to Up Holland the following day by Simon Washington, landlord of the *Old Dog Inn*, and buried in the family grave situated within the small graveyard that once surrounded the priory church. The grave already contained Nanny Lyon, his grandmother, and Elizabeth Lyon, his mother. Given George Lyon's unenviable reputation, his name was not added to the gravestone.

In the wake of the arrest, trial and execution of the likes of George Lyon and his fellow highwaymen, life at Up Holland improved immensely. The historic village was transformed into a peaceful, quiet and respectable location. However, although Lyon was dead it would appear that his spirit had not departed Up Holland. At the beginning of the twentieth century, almost a century since his execution, strange happenings occurred at his former home.

The inexplicable events culminated on Sunday 7 August 1904. His house, located next door to the once infamous *White Lion,* was now occupied by Mrs Winstanley and her four sons. One of the oldest properties in the village, it was a substantial building, three storeys high with walls three feet thick. And yet on the evening in question those walls had begun to tremble and shake, as if suffering the consequences of an earthquake.

This page and opposite:
Following his execution at Lancaster Castle on 22 April 1815, George Lyon's body was brought home to Up Holland by Simon Washington, landlord of the *Old Dog Inn*, and buried in the small priory graveyard. The family grave already contained Nanny Lyon, his grandmother, and Elizabeth Lyon, his mother, and, given George Lyon's unenviable reputation, it meant that his name was not added to the gravestone.

Rumbling and banging noises were also heard in one of the upstairs bedrooms. Closer inspection showed that the disturbances emanated from the remnants of a former window, long since bricked up (during the period when the much-despised Window Tax had resulted in many of the nation's larger houses sacrificing some of their windows in an effort to avoid or reduce the burden of taxation), now forming a recess in the bedroom.

The visitations began on an August weekend and increased in intensity night after night. Building stones vibrated so much that they became detached from the walls; shelves and cupboards crashed to the floor and items were flung across the room with great force. But once the intensity of the moment had passed, many of the 'ghostly items' returned to their original locations; and indeed, most inexplicable of all, the loose stones were not only returned to the wall, but became tight again in their crevices. A combination of the family's terror and great scepticism by the public at large caused one of the local councillors, Richard Baxter, to visit the house during the evening and sit in the 'haunted bedroom' in the hope of witnessing the phenomenon. He was not to be disappointed. Almost on cue the strange antics began and he was both alarmed and amazed. Baxter not only confirmed the reports to

George Lyon's former home, which had been the location for very strange occurrences in August 1904, was demolished thirty years later and today its former location is occupied by the car park of the once infamous *White Lion* public house.

be genuine but hired a mason to inspect the walls so as to ensure that the stones were indeed firmly set and nothing else was untoward.

Such a terrifying spectacle resulted in the family running from their home in fear. As accounts of these ungodly events spread around the neighbourhood they raised a great deal of interest, much of it macabre, resulting in large crowds gathering outside the house as nightfall came – in the ghoulish hope of witnessing what was now being referred to as 'George Lyon's poltergeist'. As matters continued, the size of the crowd outside the house increased in size, some reports estimating it to be in excess of 2,000. Having such a large mass of people assembling in a confined space soon led to a number of public order offences. The police were often called out to disperse the crowd, and to make arrests for drunkenness and lewd behaviour.

Were these strange goings on attributable to the troubled

ghost of George Lyon, the former highwayman hanged for his many crimes? We'll never know. What is known is that – despite having attracted such a sizable and devoted audience – the happenings ended as inexplicably as they had begun.

Up Holland's infamous 'haunted house' was demolished in 1934 and nothing remains of it today.

CHAPTER 18

The Case of the Hindley Collier

1904

He heard Martha cry out at the top of her voice: 'No, don't, don't!'

In 1904, although Queen Victoria had been dead for more than three years, the promise of what the new Edwardian era might bring had yet to be fulfilled. The lives of Wigan's working classes had changed little since the Victorian era – earning a living was just as hard as it had ever been, and the homes of the poorest members of society were just as horrid – there were one or two discernable changes, the most obvious being the sight of automobiles on the town's streets, and the steam-power trams had given way to the much faster electric trams. And yet, in spite of significant

St John's Methodist Church, a notable landmark in Hindley.

Hindley's Victorian Rayner Park.

improvements in the policing, Wigan still had an alarming crime rate. Most alarming of all, murder was commonplace.

Peter Turner, a twenty-four-year-old collier, had worked for the Wigan Coal & Iron Company, one of two large mining concerns in the town, for just over ten years. He lived in a humble dwelling in Bolton's Yard at Hindley, to the east of the town centre, with his common law wife, Martha. He was described as a sullen man and notably quiet by nature but was well known in the area, and respected by his fellow miners. It was something of a surprise therefore when he was charged with the wilful murder of his wife Martha.

The prosecution, led by Mr Maxwell, stated that the accused had been out drinking on the night of the murder, 20 May 1904, and had been seen frequenting a number of the local public houses. Several witnesses who gave evidence during the trial confirmed this. John Atherton, the immediate neighbour of the Turners and a fellow miner, stated that he had seen Mr Turner staggering home along the alleyway behind the houses, clearly in a drunken state, at around 10.30 pm. Shortly afterwards he had heard shouting coming from next door and then Mrs Turner had come banging on his door, screaming that her husband had thrown a lamp at her which had caused a glancing blow to the side of her head. She also claimed that he had punched and kicked her, though Atherton told the court that there was no visual evidence of that. Mrs Turner was in a highly distressed state and told Atherton that her husband had thrown her out of her home and refused to let her return. However, although Atherton had agreed to let her stay the night in his home, soon after Mr Turner came around in an angry state and

Two views of Market Street, Hindley.

began banging on the door, shouting at Atherton to bring out his wife. When Atherton had refused, Turner attempted to break down the door, and when this failed began breaking the windows. Clearly concerned for the safety of Mrs Turner, Atherton came out and reassured Peter that all was well and that if he would calm down and return home he would bring his wife back home a little later.

Later that night, after Atherton had attended to the cut on Martha Turner's head, and her husband seemingly in a much calmer state, he carried out his promise and walked Martha back to her own front door. Martha crossed the threshold first, some paces ahead of Atherton and before he could even enter the house he heard Martha cry out at the top of her voice: 'No, don't, don't!' Rushing in, Atherton found Martha lying flat on her back in a pool of blood caused by a severe wound to the head. Beside her body lay a poker. Atherton immediately knelt down beside Martha and found to his relief that she was not dead but unconscious. Atherton immediately summoned his wife from next door and together the pair of them lifted Martha off the floor and placed her in a chair where they could attend to the serious head wound.

Meanwhile, her husband simply sat in a chair, his head in his hands, crying. When challenged by Atherton as to why he had done such a thing, Peter Turner simply replied: 'I don't know.' In the meantime, Martha regained consciousness and Mrs Atherton helped her to bed. The Athertons remained in the house until things had settled and finally left at around 3 am.

The following morning, Martha rose early and went around to see her mother, Mary Ann Marsh. When questioned by Mr Maxwell, Mrs Marsh informed the court, between fits of crying and deep emotion, that soon after her daughter had arrived at her house, her husband, Peter, had also appeared in a terrible state, crying. When she had challenged him as to what had happened the night before, Peter told her that he had struck his wife over the head with a poker.

Martha Turner died later that day as a result of the wound to her head. The court heard evidence from Dr Bowran, a local general practitioner from Hindley, who, having examined Mrs Turner's body had concluded that the blow to the head could not possibly come as a result of a fall, even if her head had perhaps struck the door latch or even a nail on the way down. Dr Bowran was adamant that the injury to the head came from a weighty blow from a blunt instrument. Mr Maxwell informed the jury that the accused, although now pleading not guilty, had told his mother-in-law that he had struck his wife over the head with a poker. Equally, as Mr Atherton had walked into the house less than a minute behind Mrs Turner, upon hearing screams of 'Don't! Don't!' and there was no one else in the house except Mr Turner, then it was crystal clear that he was

Hindley Police station, which still retains its classic 'blue lamp' and, despite being part of Greater Manchester Police since 1974, it still bears the Lancashire County Police crest.

the guilty party. Nevertheless, although it appeared to be an open and shut case, the defence barrister, Mr Shawcross, attempted to paint a picture of Peter Turner as a hard working man, a loving husband, and a person with his whole life ahead of him.

The judge summed up the case for the jury and advised them to reach a decision as to whether they were convinced that Peter Turner had in fact inflicted the wound to his wife's head. The jury retired to consider the facts of the case, before returning to the court less than an hour later with a verdict of manslaughter, on the grounds that the prisoner was clearly the worse for drink when he carried out the attack on his wife. The prisoner in the dock, who had remained silent and without emotion throughout the trial, who burst into tears every time his late wife's name had been mentioned, now looked dazed and surprised, and had clearly been expecting a guilty verdict. Taking this into consideration, the judge concluded that the crime, although carried out while under the influence of an alcoholic beverage, was serious enough to warrant a term in prison of ten years.

If the accused had appeared surprised and dazed by the verdict, the family of Martha Turner, and in particular her mother, Mary Ann Marsh, having witnessed the jury explain their daughter's death as just manslaughter, and heard the judge pass what was a relatively lenient sentence, was understandably very angry, distressed and outraged, storming out of court.

CHAPTER 19

A Jilted Lover

1951

Vengeance is a dish best served cold . . .

The motives behind a murder can be as varied as the means by which the murder itself is carried out. Many murders take place as crimes of passion. When relationships turn bad, partners have affairs and when this deception is discovered an argument ensues, often leading to a fight. In the heat of the moment a fatal blow can be delivered. It's a regrettable situation that has confronted police many, many times throughout the years. Equally, revenge can be a very powerful motive for murder and, as they say 'vengeance is a dish best served cold'. However, for a jilted lover to bide his time, bear a grudge and maintain that feeling of hatred towards his former girlfriend over weeks, or in this case months, before acting is extremely rare. This is exactly what happened in the mining village of Tyldesley, on the borders of Wigan and Bolton, in 1951.

Mona Mather, a twenty-eight-year-old single girl, came from Little Hulton, a close-knit coal mining community on the outskirts of Wigan, located near to both Bolton and Manchester. A lively girl, she liked a good time and was described by her friends as being 'a terrible flirt'. She had met Jack Wright, from Tyldesley, during the summer of 1950 and the couple started going out together on a regular basis. In many ways they were an odd match, for while Mona was very gregarious and liked to be out and about every night, spending most of her time dancing in the neighbourhood music halls, Jack, a local collier, was quiet and reserved. Many of Mona's girlfriends predicted that the relationship would not last, it was simply doomed to failure. How right they were.

Despite such predictions, by the autumn of 1950 the couple were still very much together. But their apparently rock solid relationship was about to be tested to breaking point. One rainy summer's evening, while the couple were walking hand-in-hand through a local park, Mona caught sight of a former boyfriend and, despite being with Jack at the time, she could not resist going over to him and saying hello. The former lovers stood chatting for some time, while Jack stood some distance away on his own. Their conversation was intense and flowed easily, and it was obvious for all to see that they still held a 'bond' for each other. It was clear that Jack felt awkward, and the closeness and friendliness between his girlfriend and this other man made him feel all the worse. Now in an aggressive mood, Jack could stand it no longer, went over to them and insisted that it was time that he and Mona left. However, Mona stood her ground, saying that she would 'catch him up later', but in such a way that he knew that their relationship was over – as many had predicted. As Jack walked out of the park, alone and dejected, we can only imagine the evil thoughts that were in his head. For the next six months or so there was no contact between the pair, each seemingly going their separate ways, and each having got over their break-up.

Tyldesley, the mining village located on the border between Wigan and Bolton, at the turn of the century.

Tyldesley was rather like Little Hulton, a close-knit mining community, where everyone knew everyone else. The vast majority of the men who lived in or around Tyldesley worked underground in search of coal, at mines such as Wharton Hall, Howe Bridge, Lovers Lane, Nook and Cleworth. Typically, Tyldesley held organised annual fairs and celebrations where the locals could gather and let their hair down. By far the largest was the Easter Fair, held annually on Shackerley Common, situated to the north-east of the town. In 1951, Easter fell in the first weekend in April, and the Fair, referred to locally as 'The Wakes', was held over two days, Saturday and Sunday, 7 and 8 April. Literally everyone attended, numbers swelled by people from the surrounding villages and towns.

Like many of his workmates and neighbours, Jack Wright had planned to go to the Easter Fair. On the Saturday evening he met up with some of his fellow miners and, to put them in the mood, indulged in a pub crawl, visiting almost all of the local hostelries before finishing up at the *George & Dragon*, situated not far from the fairground. Unbeknown to him, Mona had also planned to visit the Easter Fair and had also been out and about in the local public houses, accompanied by her brother and sister-in-law. Mona, who was now unattached, was

Shackerley Common was the traditional location for the Tyldesley Easter Fair.

on the lookout for a date to take her to the fair and, despite her best efforts throughout the day, had so far been unsuccessful. As the evening went on she became more and more frustrated. However, as she, her brother and his wife slowly made their way towards the fairground who should she see but her former boyfriend, Jack Wright. Seemingly forgetting how she had unceremoniously dumped him in the park six months earlier, Mona ran over and flung her arms around his neck, holding him in a tight passionate embrace. The couple seemed to get on 'like a house on fire', putting the past behind them. As the evening progressed Jack and Mona said their farewells to their companions, and went off around the fairground together, walking arm in arm.

By all accounts the couple had a great time, wandering around the amusements and going on almost all of the rides. It was almost midnight when Jack offered to walk Mona home and she readily agreed. As they left, without a care in the world, anyone would have thought that they were a happy couple and perhaps very much in love. In fact one of Jack's workmates did see them leaving the fairground and would later testify that they looked 'very happy indeed'. Appearances were very deceiving, however, and although Mona might well have had love on her mind, Jack certainly did not.

Tyldesley's rural location meant that the best way of walking home to Wharton Fold, Little Hulton was 'off the beaten track', across the fields, via well-worn footpaths. Their route took them along by the railway, towards Wharton Hall Colliery. It's a secluded spot, an ideal location for lovers, but equally as ideal a location for a murderer. The couple stopped and, as Mona wrapped her arms around Jack once more, it wasn't passion that Jack was feeling towards her, but hatred. Carrying Mona into a neighbouring field, within sight of the colliery, he strangled her with her own white silk scarf. As the life slowly drained from her body and it fell limp, he stood up and quietly walked away.

Mona's body was discovered the next morning by a local miner as he crossed the field to begin his shift at the colliery at 6 am. The police were called and a murder inquiry began, led by Chief Superintendent Mercer, though much of the work was overseen by Detective Superintendent Lindsay. As her purse was intact and laying beside the body, the police could not only establish her identity, but this ruled out robbery as the motive for the murder. The fact that they could establish her identity

The footbridge over which the lovers would have crossed the Wigan & Bolton railway. And the spoil heaps of Wharton Hall Colliery which overlooks Shackerley Common close to where Mona's body was discovered.

and address meant that the murder inquiry could move very quickly indeed. Having informed her relatives, the police were soon able to establish Mona's movements on the following evening, the public houses she had visited and, most importantly, that she had met up with her ex-boyfriend, Jack Wright, who had then taken her to the Wakes Fair.

Detectives went around to his home, at 3 John Street, Tyldesley, where he lived with his elderly mother, but Jack was not in. Enquiries followed. Later that evening, Jack wandered into Tyldesley Social Club quite unaware that Mona's body had been discovered or that the police were looking for him, the news circulating around the town like wildfire. He was quite shocked when his fellow miners began teasing him with the knowledge that 'the police think that you killed Mona'. Jack soon left the club and, feeling threatened that the police were on his trail, dashed down to the railway station, where he caught a train to Manchester in a futile effort to avoid being questioned.

In the meantime, further enquiries took place around Little Hulton and Tyldesley. After interviewing Mona's many girl-friends, the police learned of the way Mona had dumped Jack months before, and as he was the last one to see her alive, concluded that he was now their chief suspect. Following his apparent disappearance, the local police circulated his description throughout the county. This tactic worked. Jack Wright was spotted on Manchester's Oxford Road railway station later

John Street – No 3 stands on the gable end closest to the camera – where Jack Wright lived with his elderly mother.

that same evening by DC Hart of the British Transport Police. The detective summoned support from the nearby police station and he was arrested on the spot.

Jack Wright was taken to a local police station and questioned at length by the Manchester detectives. Under pressure, he began to concoct an unlikely story that while he and Mona had walked around the fairground she had met two men, who were strangers to him but who she obviously knew, and she had once again dumped him and gone off with them. He told police that was the last he had seen of Mona. He went on to elaborate that she must have been walked home with either one or both of these men. Unconvinced, the detectives informed Jack Wright that he was to be transferred to Tyldesley police station for further questioning into the murder of Mona Mather. On arrival at Tyldesley police station in the early hours of Monday morning, Jack underwent further questioning. By now he was on slippery ground, his action following the news that Mona's body had been discovered had been erratic to say the least. When asked by detectives to explain why he had suddenly left the social club to catch a train to Manchester he could offer no reasonable explanation. His story of Mona going off with two men at the fair was also rubbished by police, who had subsequently spoken to local miner, Matthew Weir, Jack's workmate who had seen the couple leaving the fair arm in arm. By the end of the interrogation the detectives were convinced that they had got the right man, and Jack Wright was charged with the wilful murder of Mona Mather.

The eagerly awaited trial of Jack Wright began at the Manchester Assizes on 12 June 1951. Evidence was presented by a variety of witnesses, including the Warrington-based pathologist, Dr Carragher, who had examined the body at the murder scene and later conducted the autopsy. He confirmed that Mona Mather had been strangled by her own scarf, and that the ligature had been pulled so tight and with so much ferocity that it had crushed her windpipe and fractured her thyroid bone.

Wright's defence counsel, led by J Robertson Crichton, interviewed their client at length during the intervening months and reached the conclusion that there was no line of defence open to them but to enter a plea of 'guilty by means of insanity'. Wright confessed to the murder of Mona Mather in the witness box, explaining that it had been more than just a crime of passion, but a wilful act of revenge following the way she had

The eagerly awaited trial of Jack Wright began at the Manchester Assizes on 12 June 1951.

not just dumped him but humiliated him. However, defence counsel also informed the court that since the break-up their client had been acting in a strange and often vengeful mood, and had actually attacked a number of women in the area – though had not gone so far as to attempt to murder any of them. They added that on Saturday 7 April he had left home with the intention to, as he had put it, 'kill a woman', and that the chance meeting with his former lover had offered him the opportunity to combine this murderous desire with that of revenge.

The prosecution, led by Mr Nelson, countered that the murder of Mona Mather had been all about revenge, and that the insanity plea was merely a smokescreen. They called several doctors who had had the opportunity to examine Jack Wright, either during his period of custody by the police or the time he had spent on remand at Manchester's Strangeways prison. Without exception, all of them concluded that in their expert opinion there was nothing to suggest that the prisoner was insane. The prosecution therefore called on the jury to dismiss the argument that the accused had not been responsible for his actions, but instead had acted in revenge when he strangled Mona Mather to death on the day in question.

The jury retired to deliberate and after less than three hours returned a guilty verdict. Justice Oliver donned his black cap and informed the prisoner that he would be taken from the court to a place of execution where he would be hanged by the neck until he was dead – for the wilful and premeditated murder of the twenty-eight-year-old Mona Mather. Thirty-two-year-old Jack Wright was executed by hanging at Manchester's Strangeways prison on the morning of 3 July 1951.

Chapter 20

A Child Murderer

1955

Two young boys have already been stabbed to death in the Wigan district. Your help may prevent another boy from being murdered

Murderers come in all shapes and sizes, and carry out their crimes for a variety of motives. It's a well known fact that many killers are known to their victims – often they are a relative or family friend. The murderous stranger, who seemingly selects his victims at random, without a reason or motive, is statistically rare, though much more sinister. Of all the murderers, the random serial killer strikes the greatest fear in the hearts of the general public, and of those, the one who focuses his attention on young children has to be regarded as the most heinous. Indeed, although the police, whilst doing their duty come in contact with a wide variety of murderers, without doubt they despise the child murderer most of all.

This most shocking crime came to haunt the inhabitants of Wigan during the middle 1950s, when the town was being stalked by a man whose victims were innocent young boys. From all appearances, his attacks were completely unprovoked and motiveless; and chosen at random. The police had little to go on, and yet what they feared from the outset, was that from the level of aggression used in the initial non-fatal attack, the perpetrator was determined to kill a young boy.

The first victim was seven-year-old William Mitchell. The young lad had initially been happily playing alongside the Leeds & Liverpool Canal with his mates, though later had wandered off on his own, perhaps to explore a quieter section of the waterway. He was approached by a man, who he would later describe to police as having blonde hair 'so light that it was almost white'. The man spoke to William momentarily before suddenly pulling out a knife and stabbing him in the chest. It was more by luck than judgement that young William managed to survive this unprovoked attack, and his description of the

The section of the Leeds & Liverpool Canal at Ince where William Mitchell was attacked while out playing.

man to the local police was of great use. Nevertheless, although a major incident inquiry was launched immediately, and many of the local 'misfits' were questioned by police, the attacker was never found. Apart from the vivid description, the detectives had little to go on and soon the trail ran cold.

However, it would not be long before the man would strike again, and although William Mitchell had been fortunate to survive this horrific attack, his next victim was less lucky. William Harmer, Billy to his mates, was just eleven years old when he suffered a frenzied and fatal attack on 27 August 1954. He had been playing alone, and his heavily bloodstained body was discovered in a field just off Miry Lane, not far from his home at 1 Vere Street.

The local police launched an extensive murder inquiry, calling on officers from other Lancashire towns, including St Helens and Oldham. Nevertheless, in spite of the extra manpower, Wigan's Chief Constable, Paul Foster, concluded that it was beyond their capabilities and he would be forced to call on the resources of Scotland Yard, who despatched a thirty-strong murder detective team to Wigan, led by Superintendent MacDougall and Detective Inspector Davies. Immediately realising the obvious similarities with the earlier attack upon William Mitchell, the police began to not only carry out house-to-house inquires in the area but re-interview all of the witnesses from the earlier incident. Despite extensive enquiries, the police were still without the hint of a possible suspect for the attacks.

An inquest was convened by J Hopwood, the Wigan coroner. Dr G B Manning, a Home Office consultant pathologist, who had carried out a post-mortem on the body of Billy Harmer, informed the court that the boy had been stabbed a total of eleven times (ten to the torso and once to the throat) from a small, single-bladed knife, possibly a penknife. He concluded that death had resulted from 'haemorrhage and shock from multiple injuries to the chest and abdomen'.

For almost a year there was no real progress. And then, during the evening of Easter Monday, 11 April 1955, the attacker struck again. This time the victim was ten-year-old Norman Yates. He had been at home that evening playing dominoes. His mother had begun to prepare a meal when her husband had returned home from work, only to discover that she had run short of sugar and had sent Norman to fetch some from a relative, Alice Yates, who lived on nearby Hope Street.

It's thought that Norman chose to use the back alley, a

The field off Miry Lane, where the body of William Harmer was discovered on 27 August 1954, is now an industrial estate.

popular shortcut, as around 9.40 pm residents heard a 'long and drawn out scream' coming from the rear of the terraced houses, so loud in fact that it could easily be heard above their television and radio sets. Jimmy Jones, who had been listening to an episode of Perry Mason, had been so disturbed by the ear-piercing scream that he immediately grabbed a bicycle lamp and ran outside into the darkness to see what had happened. He was soon joined by his neighbour, Walter Wiggins. At first neither of the men could see anything, then as Mr Jones scanned his torch beam around the waste ground they discovered the body of a young boy 'bleeding terribly'. Realising that the boy was still alive, Mr Jones ran to the local telephone box on the corner of the street to summon an ambulance. In the meantime, Mr Wiggins ran to the home of the local GP, Dr Murphy, who lived nearby. Although Norman Yates was still breathing when he had initially been found he was pronounced 'dead on arrival' by the time the ambulance reached Wigan Infirmary.

Once again, witnesses informed the police that they had seen a tall man, very thin and with almost white hair, aged in his mid-twenties, running away from the area around the time of the incident. It was later discovered that Norman lived in nearby Heywood Street, and his terribly distraught mother confirmed that he had only left home to fetch some sugar, and had been gone less

This page and opposite:
Hope Street, where Alice Yates lived, had been Norman Yates's destination on the evening of Monday 11 April 1955, though he never reached there as he was savagely attacked on waste ground located off Cross Street. The area has seen massive re-development since the 1950s and the only building that survives from the time of the murder is the chapel on the corner of Cross Street and Hope Street.

than ten minutes. A closer examination of the young boy's body revealed that he had been stabbed a total of four times, mainly clustered around the chest, though the fatal blow had been a cut to his throat.

Chief Superintendent Lindsay was placed in charge of what was now a major murder inquiry. These attacks had sent fear into the local population, and the police seized on this by distributing pamphlets stating: 'Two young boys have already been stabbed to death in the Wigan district. Your help may prevent another boy from being murdered.' The police were flooded with responses, and many names of potential suspects came forward. Indeed, several men were bought in for questioning, including a former inmate of a Liverpool-based asylum who had recently relocated to Wigan, though in the end all of the suspects were released without charge. However, despite what had been described as a 'very good start', the inquiry once again ran cold. One by one the positive leads became dead ends, and information from the public began to fade.

Although Lindsay had in many ways been disappointed by the lack of solid leads, several names had been put forward by the general public as potential suspects. Amongst them was 'Norman Green', who had been suggested as a suspect on more than one occasion during the investigation, but he had initially been excluded from the investigation on the grounds that he was not local to Wigan. Green originated from Aberdeen, and although he had lived in Wigan for almost fifteen years by the time of the murders, he still retained his Scottish accent, and none of the witnesses, including Billy Harmer, had mentioned this. In spite of this obvious setback, further investigations were carried out which made Green look more interesting to the police. For example, he had failed to qualify for National Service on the grounds that he had defective eyesight and, more importantly, he had been classified as being 'of an emotionally unstable character'. With this, Chief Superintendent Lindsay came to the conclusion that it would be wise to bring Green in for questioning.

The following morning, Friday 15 April, DS Edmundson and DS Parkinson arrested Green at the local corn millers, Charlsons & Sons, where he was employed as a labourer. He was escorted to Lower Ince police station where the murder detectives were able to question him at length over the murder of the two young boys. At first, Green denied being in

Lower Ince over the bank holiday, and even offered a very detailed and in some ways, very convincing account of his movements during the weekend. However, as the interview became more intense, and as the detectives began to question his actions more closely, his story began to break up. Green began to concoct a new account of his movements over the bank holiday weekend, suggesting that he had in fact been in Lower Ince, but he had spent much of his time drinking in the *Railway Hotel.*

Not satisfied with his explanation of events, Edmundson and Parkinson suspended the interview and decided to search Green's home on Hallgate, where they found several interesting items that might be connected to the case, including a navy blue suit that had suspicious stains on the front. The detectives despatched all of the items removed from Green's home to the forensic laboratory for immediate analysis, while they resumed the interview with Green. This second interview proved much more satisfactory. By now Norman Green had been in custody for several hours and had time to think of the predicament he was in. Now, confronted with the knowledge that his home had been searched and items of interest to the police were now receiving forensic examination, Green cracked and confessed to the murders, saying in the case of Norman Yates: 'I'm so sorry for his mother.'

Norman Green provided the police with a full and detailed account of the events of Easter Monday. He had been drinking in the *Railway Hotel* and had remained there until about 9 pm. He went on to say that he used the public toilet at the rear of the public house and so left by the back door into the alleyway, where he had caught sight of a young boy hurrying along the street. As the young lad had entered the alleyway, perhaps making a short cut, Green had stopped him and asked where he could obtain a drink of water. The boy had offered to take him to his mother's house, though as Green followed him out of the alleyway and across some wasteland Green had stabbed the boy.

Norman Yates was buried on Friday 15 April. Thousands of people turned out to watch the funeral cortège as it made its way to Westwood Cemetery, and Norman's former school mates lined the streets. Later that evening, as rumours began to circulate throughout the town that the police had arrested someone for his murder there was great excitement. The news spread like wildfire around the town, and a rowdy crowd

Norman Yates was buried in Westwood Cemetery on Friday 15 April and, later that day, Chief Superintendent Lindsay informed a large and volatile crowd outside Ince police station that a 'twenty-three-year-old man was helping them with their enquiries'.

gathered outside the local police station eager to hear the rumour confirmed. In an effort to ease the tension and avert any potential public disorder occurring, Chief Superintendent Lindsay came out and addressed the crowd, confirming that 'a twenty-three-year-old local man was now helping the police with their enquiries into the murders of William Harmer and Norman Yates, and indeed the earlier attack upon William Mitchell'. Later that evening, just after 8 pm, Chief Superintendent Lindsay went outside again and this time informed the waiting crowd that the suspect, one Norman William Green, had just been charged with the murder of Norman Yates, and that he would be appearing before Wigan magistrates early the following morning.

Having provided the detectives with a full confession, Norman Green accompanied them back to Charlson & Sons on Dawber Street to point out where he had stashed the murder weapon. Hidden in a secluded corner of the workshop and wrapped in a piece of old sacking was a bloodstained knife with a long, thin blade. Norman Green was returned to Lower Ince police station, spending a night in the cells, and on the following morning, prior to appearing before the magistrates he was interviewed by DI Davies who had led the inquiry into the earlier murder of William Harmer.

When Green appeared in front of the magistrates the following morning, the charge had been altered to include the murder of William Harmer and the earlier attack upon William Mitchell. However, by the time of the committal proceedings on 13 May 1955, the second indictment of the wilful murder of eleven-year-old William Harmer on 27 August 1954 (which Green had already confessed to) had been dropped, though the matter would be held on file, and he was summoned to stand trial at the next Manchester Assizes for the wilful murder of Norman Yates.

The trial, before Justice Oliver, began on 2 July 1955 and took only three days to complete. Despite his full and frank confession, Green's defence counsel, led by J D Robertson Crichton QC, entered a plea of insanity, which they maintained throughout the trial. Although it was clear from his confession that Norman Green was the murderer of William Harmer and Norman Yates, the defence played on the fact that the murders had been so horrific and without motive that it could only have been committed by someone who was clearly insane. A full medical assessment had by now been carried out on Norman

Detective Sergeants Edmundson and Parkinson searched the home of their prime suspect, Norman Green, on Hallgate.

Green and had concluded that he was 'both mentally and emotionally immature and a sexual deviant'.

On 5 July, with the case for both the prosecution and defence now concluded, Mr Justice Oliver summed up and the jury, comprising ten men and two women, who had followed the trial intently throughout, retired to the jury room to consider their verdict at just after 3 pm. Having been away for less than four hours, the jury returned to the court and informed Mr Justice Oliver that they were still unable to reach a verdict as they were having difficulty ascertaining whether Green was sane or insane at the time of the murder. The judge told them that it was their decision and their decision alone to determine Green's level of sanity, though he did clarify the point by adding that, in all probabilities, a person should be deemed sane rather than insane. Once more the jury retired to consider their verdict, though the judge did add that if they were unable to reach a verdict he would not be inclined to detain them any longer than necessary. Within a quarter of an hour the jury returned, and delivered a verdict of 'guilty as charged'.

Justice Oliver, having donned his black cap, passed sentence on Norman Green, now visibly trembling in the dock. Having been asked whether he had anything to add as to why a judgement of death should not be passed on him, Norman Green replied 'no'. Justice Oliver informed him that he would be taken from this place to a point of execution and 'hanged by the neck until dead'.

Although his defence counsel did not appeal the verdict, they did petition the Home Office for a reprieve, again on the grounds that their client was insane. The Home Secretary reviewed the case notes but reached a conclusion that there was no reason for him to interfere in the verdict, so the reprieve was rejected. Norman Green, aged twenty-three, was hanged at Walton Prison by the noted executioner, Albert Pierrepoint, on Wednesday 27 July 1955. Within Wigan, most people concluded that justice had been done, and that Norman Green had gone to the gallows not only for the murder of Norman Yates to which he was found guilty, but the murder of William Harmer and the attack upon William Mitchell.

Index